The following are the opinions of people who have read *Posh and Friends* in manuscript form:

A most remarkable, unexpected and charming book, which I read with pleasure. Part dog-oriented memoir, and part practical guide for dog-owners and dog-lovers, I am sure it will have broad appeal.

– Michael Spicer, former Anglo American executive.

Denis Worrall has an incredible memory of all the dogs in his life and his personal reminiscences of them are quite charming. Congratulations! It could become a best-seller.

– John Scott, former editor of *The Cape Times*.

I very much enjoyed reading *Posh and Friends*. It is entertaining and informative and will be of real value to dog-lovers all over. I like the fact that Denis has written it not just for South African readers but for Australian and UK readers. This is a fascinating read.

– Dave Gant former political associate of Denis Worrall.

As the  tify with and appreciat htful book!

/Iark Nowitz.

Posh and Friends will give huge insight and delight to dog-lovers everywhere!

– Gisele Vanderstraeten, architect.

This is a gem of a book and a great gift for dog-lovers. *Posh and Friends* is much more than a dog-lovers guide to bringing up happy dogs. The companionship dogs give, especially to ageing dog-lovers, is described with extraordinary sensitivity. Once published, *Posh and Friends* will be the best gift anybody can give an elderly relative or friend with a dog.

– Sharon Worrall, former advertising agency boss.

Thank you for letting me read your manuscript. I consider it a compliment. Denis, you have done a beautiful job in bringing out your experience of dogs. It is heart-warming to read. And I enjoyed all your quotes and the poetry. One quote in particular that I like very much is the one by EB White about dogs today being fed on scraped beef and vitamin B1 and living in bed with you. That is how my wife Jilly treats **two** of our **eight** Shi-Zhus! Denis, you've written a rare and charming book. It will surely delight dog-lovers in South Africa and beyond!

– Gunter Steffens, director of companies who served in International banks in Frankfurt and London

POSH

AND FRIENDS

A DOG-LOVER'S GUIDE TO HAPPY DOGS

By
Dr Denis Worrall

GreenShootsBooks
Cape Town, South Africa

ISBN 978-0-620-96104-2 Print

eISBN 978-0-620-96105-9 e-Book

Sula Book Distributors
Suzette Hamman Ph: 083 290 7576
suzette@sula.co.za
Also available on Amazon as a Kindle
eBook and paper book

Layout and cover design by Boutique Books
Printed in South Africa by Digital Action

DEDICATION

This book is dedicated to Posh and the millions of homeless dogs, and to those individuals and organisations who make a difference.

FOREWORD BY DAVID POTTER

This book is a delightful mixture of man, family and dog and draws out how each can reinforce the other. All of this is laced with interesting, unusual and amusing poetry and anecdotes. It includes much practical wisdom and guidance. It will also serve as a vibrant reminder to all those who love dogs why they do so. To those who do not have a dog and no intention of getting one, Denis Worrall's endearing book might even change their mind.

– David Potter is a former banker, including with Investec, and a former Trustee of the Nelson Mandela Fund in the UK.

CONTENTS

LIST OF POEMS

I have enjoyed poetry from an early age and with growing respect for dogs have come to appreciate the increasing body of international poetry celebrating dogs from a human point of view. Quite frankly, it would be unthinkable to produce a volume like *Posh and Friends* without some acknowledgement of the comfort, joy and, yes, the pain our four-footed friends cause us and not express our thanks to the poets whose creative genius made this possible. *Denis Worrall*

POSH AND FRIENDS

A DOG-LOVER'S GUIDE TO HAPPY DOGS

By

Dr Denis Worrall

Academic, Advocate and Former Ambassador to Australia and the Court of St James.

About Man's Best Friend

Dogs aren't the most numerous of our pets, but they arguably are the most important. Apart from its practical uses, from seeing-eye to sheep herder to property guard, the dog has a positive, therapeutic psychological effect on the human beings around it. Stroking a dog lowers heart rate and blood pressure. Company of a faithful canine friend is known to aid convalescence in the sick. And, because of the dog's need for regular exercise, it helps keep its master fit into the bargain.
— Dr David Taylor, BVMS.

VALIDATION

 Dr Denis Worrall and his dog Posh have been a client and patient in my practice for several years. From the beginning it was very clear that Dr Worrall was keenly interested in "his" Posh and clearly took good care of her. I was therefore very pleased to hear that he was writing this book as I realised it would be different from most of the self-help books that are available in that the advice given would be thoroughly researched and related back to real-life experiences. Advice from experienced dog-owners is always invaluable, and that is certainly the case with Dr Worrall and Posh. I have found his research and advice sound, well-expressed and caring, and I thank him for inviting me to proofread the script from a professional point of view.

Sincerely,

Dr Paul Bernhardi | BVSc. BSc (Agric) Hon. - Blue Cross Veterinary Hospital

POSH

AND FRIENDS

CHAPTER 1

BY WAY OF EXPLANATION

That I have written a manual or guidebook for dog-lovers, when I am neither a vet nor any sort of dog trainer, some would say requires an explanation – which I gladly offer. Dogs have been an important part of every aspect of what most people would say has been a rather diverse career. That is why Posh, the book, is written the way it is and I naturally hope you enjoy reading it and find it helpful in bringing up happy and healthy dogs.

The world is said to be divided between dog-lovers and cat-lovers and my family has always been a dog family. I remember in my very early years a fox terrier called Mickey, but the others that followed - Scotty and then Bonzo - were non-descript. My family background encouraged an interest in dogs. In fact, I have a vivid recollection of my mother recounting to me the story of *Jock of The Bushveld*, Sir James Percy Fitzpatrick's classic novel published in 1907, about the miners and transporters in the gold-digging days of the late 19th century and which I recently delved into again. The character I found most striking is less Jock than his mother Jess and that passage describing how she protected her litter:

It was dark when Ted her master returned to the wagon. She jumped up at his chest giving a long tremulous whimper of welcome, then ran straight ahead to the nesting in the grass. He took a lantern and we followed but not too close. When he knelt down to look at the puppies, she stayed over them and pushed herself in between him and them; when he put out a hand to touch them, she pushed it away with her nose, whining softly in protest and trembling with excitement – you could see she would not bite, but she hated him to touch her puppies. Finally, when he picked one up, she gave a low cry and caught his wrist gently, but held it. That was Jess, the mother of Jock.

So, I experienced dogs from an early age. But my wife Anita's experience was different in this regard, having been born and spending her early years in war-ravaged Romania, followed by relatively short residences in Israel and Havana, Cuba, before settling in Montréal, Canada. We met in the US as post-graduate students at Cornell University, she in psychology and me in political science. We fell in love, decided to marry and settled in South Africa.

OUR FIRST DOG COMES TO US

As young marrieds living in Durban I am sure we thought of having a dog – especially given that several of our married friends had dogs – but, with both of us working and as apartment dwellers, we didn't think it was practical.

The opportunity arose after I'd been appointed to the University of the Witswatersrand and we bought a house in the Johannesburg suburb of Linden. And then it happened in an extraordinary way. One morning, quite early, a dog came dashing up our driveway and literally collapsed in the garage. She was a relatively young dog, a boxer, and clearly exhausted with a couple of slight wounds on her face. My theory was that she had been running loose and was hit by a car somewhere higher up in the estate and had taken off in a frenzy. She was a lovely animal and Anita took to her immediately. We therefore didn't hesitate to make her feel at home and naming her Mandy. In fact, we have a photo of our son Chris in his nappy, drinking a bottle and using Mandy's tummy as his pillow!

I suppose we should have advertised the dog's whereabouts in a local shopwindow or newspaper, but we didn't. However, I was faced with a very definite moral issue three weeks or so after she had made her home with us. I used to run most evenings around a nearby soccer field with Mandy keeping pace with me. One evening, I saw a man and a young boy standing on the side of the field clearly gesticulating to and calling the dog. It obviously crossed my mind that these could be the original owners but right there and then I decided to let the dog decide. If she stayed with me, as she did for several more laps, and the strangers went away, as they eventually did, she was ours.

And that is exactly what happened. She was ours for some thirteen happy years, living with us in Grahamstown when I was appointed to the Institute of Social and Economic Research at Rhodes, and subsequently in Cape Town when I went to parliament.

OUR FIRST HOME IN THE MOTHER CITY

Our house in Cape Town was high up on Molteno Road in Oranjezicht, with a superb view of the city and Table Bay and yet close enough to the pipetrack running along the mountain slope for it to be easily accessible for jogs and runs, accompanied of course by Mandy. It was a very happy home to which she made a substantial contribution. The choice of Oranjezicht was fortuitous because in a by-election in 1977 I won the parliamentary seat of Cape Town Gardens, which included Oranjezicht, with a handy majority over both the Progressive and the United Party candidates. It was an election in which Anita's cosmopolitan and cultural background, and the fact that her child psychology practice was in the constituency, made a big contribution.

My parents had retired to Gordons Bay, **a sea-resort** that is close to Cape Town, and made available to us a house that was almost on the beach and which was ours whenever we wanted it. And that was often, because we got a lot of enjoyment out of it. But the real beneficiary in a way was Mandy. She would run down the beach and into the waves and swim out way beyond the breakers. As our son Dean reminded me, after swimming for half an hour or so she would come back to the beach to pee and then return to the sea! At one point she was so far out in the bay that NSRI, obviously quite unnecessarily, sent a boat to fetch her. That was Mandy.

THE DOGS AT LIVE OAK BEACH, SANTA CRUZ

BY ALICIA OSTRIKER, AN AMERICAN
AWARD-WINNING FEMINIST POET

As if there could be a world
Of absolute innocence
In which we forget ourselves

The owners throw sticks
And half-bald tennis balls
Toward the surf
And the happy dogs leap after them
As if catapulted—

Black dogs, tan dogs,
Tubes of glorious muscle—

Pursuing pleasure
More than obedience
They race, skid to a halt in the wet sand,
Sometimes they'll plunge straight into
The foaming breakers

Like diving birds, letting the green turbulence
Toss them, until they snap and sink

Teeth into floating wood
Then bound back to their owners
Shining wet, with passionate speed
For nothing,
For absolutely nothing but joy.

CHAPTER 2

A NEW LIFE IN AUSTRALIA

What all this says is that our family life in Cape Town at that time was a very happy one and we weren't exactly overjoyed when in 1982 the government invited me to be South African ambassador to Australia. It was not an easy decision. I was really enjoying becoming increasingly involved in the President's Council and its challenges, while at the same time maintaining an advocate's practice.

Anita, in turn, was developing her practice and the boys were happily in schools of their choice. To be fair, we didn't really know much about Australia as a society and except for the occasional diplomat we didn't know many Australians. The Foreign Minister sweetened the offer by suggesting that en route to Australia I would spend a month gaining experience in our New York Diplomatic Mission and that Anita and the boys would meet me in New York and then go from there to Montréal, so visiting Anita's family. Then together we would fly to Los Angeles, and from there to Taiwan, as the Taiwan government, with whose representatives in South Africa I had good relations, had invited us to make an official visit to that country. After that, on to Canberra.

It was an understanding between the Foreign Minister and me that, if I accepted the position in Canberra, I could expect to be appointed ambassador in London as soon as that posting became available. At the time, it was South Africa's top posting.

MANY ISSUES TO BE RESOLVED

This major change in our family circumstances naturally involved many questions and many different issues to be resolved, not the least of which was, of course, the schooling of our boys and Anita's practice. And tucked in there was the question, "What about Mandy?" Now a gracious old lady, could we inflict on her a long airflight (which must be a horrid experience for a dog, or any animal for that matter!) followed by six months quarantine in some or other home for lost dogs on the outskirts of Canberra?

The answer was obviously negative, and an arrangement was made to keep Mandy within the family by asking one of the grannies to take care of her. This was, quite frankly, not the best of arrangements. This was borne out by one of the first calls we received on arrival in Canberra, telling us that Mandy had passed on. I never pressed for details, guessing that my mother, in her wisdom, was responsible. But Anita quickly organised a mock funeral in the garden and she and the boys didn't waste any time in visiting the SPCA.

TWO DOGS RATHER THAN ONE

The South African Embassy and residence in Canberra, not unlike other countries represented there, occupy very spacious grounds, and after a couple of trips with the boys Anita decided we could accommodate two dogs rather than one. And so it was that she and the boys chose Lucy, a mutt, and named her Lucifer because she was black, and Woden, a male Labrador. Woden in classical mythology is the god of war but it is also the name of a major shopping centre in Canberra. Anita says Woden was called Woden **with** a capital W as a way of placating me, because I had insisted on only one dog!

Anita describes how Woden came about. They had already decided on Lucy when Chris came running up. "Mommy, Mommy come see this Labrador puppy!" which she did and that's how it was two dogs and not one.

Neither were what one would describe as pure bred, but both were delightful animals and fitted easily into the diplomatic milieu. South African embassy dinner parties, aside from all other considerations, became known for the dogs in the receiving line or under the table and accompanying the ambassador at the dawn of the working day across the lawn from the residence to the back door of the Chancery, with his last cup of breakfast coffee in his hand.

Incidentally, not all diplomatic and consular posts have spacious offices or land, and pets and dogs in particular were in my time highly controversial. I remember a Heads of Mission meeting called in Pretoria when there was a special item on the agenda referring to damage to property caused by diplomatic pets. And when it came up, I looked across at the late but fondly-remembered Frikkie Botha, who was our very successful ambassador in Japan, where I had visited him. The damage caused by his dogs was visible all over the residence. But like the perfect diplomat, he kept a straight face.

CHAPTER 3

THE LUCKY COUNTRY

Back in Canberra, with my appointment to London now a reality, the time had come to say goodbye to our many friends among the public and, given the country's apartheid image, the surprisingly many contacts also among the diplomatic corps.

When I had presented my credentials to the Dean of the Diplomatic Corps, the Netherlands Ambassador Emile Schiff, my staff had told me in Canberra, if it is to be at 11 o'clock it is 11 o'clock and so it was that I arrived precisely on time and he was waiting for me at the front door. And his first words to me were: "Welcome to Canberra, colleague! Tennis or golf?" I did get to play regular tennis with both the Russian and the French ambassadors, and the Hungarian and Polish ambassadors became fishing buddies in the celebrated man-made lake Burley Griffin.

The American residence was directly opposite us, and I got to know the American ambassador Robert Dillon very well. He had the habit when introducing me to anybody of saying: "Like me, Denis is a political appointee. What's a political appointee? Somebody whose friends don't want him in the Cabinet but whom the President will employ, provided it's outside the country!" Incidentally, my friend, who had been appointed by

President Reagan, owned the biggest Cadillac dealership in California!

By the middle of March, I had made and received courtesy calls from over 60 ambassadors. Many of their countries were not on friendly terms with South Africa, but in Canberra you needed to be friends with everybody because you didn't know whom you would be sitting next to at a dinner party or sharing a barbecue given by a local who didn't take political differences between countries seriously.

Donald Horne's book about Australia – *The Lucky Country* – was actually intended as a critique. But Australians have adopted it as a nickname for the country, and they are right in describing it so because Australia is that – a lucky country. Aside from having enormous commodity wealth, its 24 million people live in the thirteenth wealthiest country in the world with the ninth highest per capita income, and the second highest human development index globally. The country therefore ranks high in quality of life, health, education, economic freedom, civil liberties and political rights. And what political issues do arise lend themselves to solutions.

Anita, aside from being very active on behalf of the Embassy and within the diplomatic community, had been asked to be vice-president of the Women's International Club of Canberra – a significant achievement that reflected her linguistic versatility and close relationship in particular with the wives in the smaller non-English speaking missions. She was also using her spare time to complete a postgraduate course in special education at Canberra University.

Aside from the more formal goodbyes, we had invited our Australian friends, our boys' schools **and diplomats from all embassies to several showings of Jamie Uys' superb movie** *Funny People*, and they came in droves.

But the move to London involved some difficult decisions: which of the non-permanent staff would we take with us? And, again, that heartrending question about dogs. Both deserved to go with us, but in the final analysis we could only take one, and that was to be Woden. Our choice of a foster family for Lucy was careful. The last sight we had of her was looking out of the open window of a minibus, accompanied by a happy family of six children. Our choice of a local staff member to go to London was Ali, a young and energetic Iranian who was an excellent cook, had good relations with the boys and fondly looked after the dogs. Ali, with his young Australian wife and child, was delighted to accept. And it was Ali who thought of putting Lyndon's unwashed rugby socks in Woden's crate for the air flight to London.

MORGAN'S DOG

BY ANDREW BARTON PATERSON, AUSTRALIAN POET

(BETTER KNOWN AS 'BANJO' *WWW.POETRYLIBRARY.EDU.AU*

Morgan the drover explained,
As he drank from his battered quart-pot,
Many a slut I have trained;
This is the best of the lot.
Crossing these stringybark hills,
Hungry and rocky and steep
This is the country that kills
Weakly and sore-footed sheep.

Those that are healthy and strong
Battle away in the lead,
Carting the others along,
Eating the whole of the feed.

That's where this little red slut
Shows you what's bred in the bone;
Works it all out in her nut,
Handles it all on her own.

Backwards and forwards she'll track,
Gauging the line at a glance,
Keeping the stronger ones back,
Giving the tailers a chance.

Posh and Friends

Weary and hungry and lame,
Sticking all day to her job,
Thin as a rabbit, but game,
Working in front of the mob.

Tradesmen, I call 'em, the dogs,
Those that'll work in a yard;
Bark till they're hoarser than frogs,
Makin' 'em savage and hard.

Others will soldier and shirk
While there's a rabbit to hunt:
This is an artist at work;
Watch her -- out there -- in the front.

Australia has a dog population of 4.8 million and therefore a pet ownership ratio similar to the US, where 65% of homes which have dogs. This is more than the UK with 40%. South Africa has nine million dogs, 85% of which are estimated to be in townships. The pet ownership in New Zealand is 75%.

CHAPTER 4

PETS AND LONDON

As most people know, London is not an easy place to keep dogs – even small dogs. As in all big cities, apartments are the dominant residential mode, leaving pavements and some public parks the only place to exercise your dog, **on condition you pick up its droppings and** accept being penalised for failing to do so. The result is that if you walk your dog you go with a poop-scoop or lots of special plastic bags.

We have two sons living in London and in a playful way the question divided **one of them on whether to get a dog or not. My son and the two children** were in favour, my daughter-in-law not. Why? I asked her. "Because I know who is going to have to do the work. The picking up!" Since then, the matter has been resolved but I haven't asked whether in that debate John Sparrow's description of a dog in London featured: "That indefatigable and unsavoury engine of pollution – the dog!"

LOST DOG

BY ELLEN BASS

AMEICAN POET AND CO-AUTHOR OF THE COURAGE TO HEAL.

It's just getting dark, fog drifting in,
damp grasses fragrant with anise and mint,
and though I call his name
until my voice cracks,
there's no faint tinkling
of tag against collar, no sleek
black silhouette with tall ears rushing
toward me through the wild radish.

As it turns out, he's trotted home,
tracing the route of his trusty urine.
Now he sprawls on the deep red rug, not dead,
not stolen by a car on West Cliff Drive.

Every time I look at him, the wide head
resting on outstretched paws,
joy does another lap around the racetrack
of my heart. Even in sleep
when I turn over to ease my bad hip,
I'm suffused with contentment.

If I could lose him like this every day
I'd be the happiest woman alive.

WODEN IN LONDON

The South African ambassadorial residence is something of an exception. It is situated in very spacious grounds, and includes an all-weather tennis court which is something unique in central London and which I used regularly. (A frequent singles partner was the late Donald Gordon.) So Woden would enjoy all the space he required and the attentions of Ali after he had completed six months of quarantine in Staines, near to Heathrow Airport, where we visited him virtually every Saturday until his joyful release. And his release came with him doing a somersault and, on arrival at the residence, inspecting virtually all 40 rooms before settling into the laundry.

Ali, who it will be remembered was with us in Canberra, was generally fond of dogs but particularly fond of Woden and, aside from the parks and greens in close vicinity to Highveld, he took him walking on main streets and our sons approvingly say – not that I believe for one moment the dog could have enjoyed it – even into Harrod's and on the subway.

However, from a diplomatic point of view his residence was uneventful, except for one small ripple toward the end of our term. In fact, it happened at one of the bigger farewell dinner parties we gave in the residence. We had a piano and the well-known soprano Elizabeth Harwood, who had become a good friend of Anita's, offered to perform on the occasion – an offer we were very pleased to accept.

She was seated during the meal next to another good friend, a well-known Arab gentleman, and opposite him was his wife. It seems that Woden had been moving among the seated legs and brushed himself quite vigorously against the Arab gentleman who, out of the side of his mouth, told his wife, apparently with concern, that the singer was feeling him up!

CHAPTER 5

PRESSURE FOR SANCTIONS GROWS

My arrival in London more or less coincided with the increase of pressure for sanctions against South Africa. In fact, Prime Minister Margaret Thatcher remarks in her memoirs, "The year 1985 was one of mounting crises for South Africa."

Notwithstanding some positive developments on the Labour Relations front, and the introduction of the President's Council, demonstrations, protests and mass actions were widespread, with the government clamping down with restrictions on movement and so on. Internationally, the result was increasing demands for sanctions. Thatcher and her government were against sanctions.

Aside, obviously, from protecting UK business interests, which had a significant involvement in South Africa, she believed apartheid would be defeated by maintaining contact with South Africa and keeping up pressure on the South African government and by growing the economy. Harry Oppenheimer put it like this: "Apartheid is to keep people apart, but sustained growth brings them together." Most business people in South Africa shared this view.

As Ambassador, this obviously was also my position and I was able to claim the support of three very prominent political liberals who were against sanctions, namely Alan Paton, the author of *Cry the Beloved Country*, Mangosuthu Buthelezi, head of the major black political party at that time, and Helen Suzman, who for a long time was the lone member of the Progressive Federal Party in Parliament and probably the strongest critic of apartheid within the South African political system.

PRESIDENT BOTHA AND THE RUBICON SPEECH

While supporting the UK Government's position, something Lord Charles Powell, Foreign Affairs Private Secretary to Prime Minister Thatcher acknowledged when he said, "while Thatcher took over direction of policy in South Africa with some help from me, Ambassador Denis Worrall was an invaluable source of information of debates within the SA government". And Foreign Secretary Geoffrey Howe acknowledged my role in his biography when he wrote of "the excellent and liberal South African Ambassador".

While being as helpful as I could be to the British government, I was also pressing the South African government to make the changes that it had promised to make. President PW Botha was supposed to deliver what so many people expected in the so-called "Rubicon Speech", but this was universally seen as a disaster. It strengthened the case for sanctions. For me personally, it acutely raised the question of whether I could not serve my country better than by being in London.

Following my resignation as **a**mbassador and my decision to contest the expected general election of 1987 as an independent candidate in opposition to the governing party, I returned to South Africa, leaving Anita to complete the packing of our personal belongings and manage the end of our boys' schooling in the UK. And when they came to South Africa, Woden was on the same flight and Anita tells how she and the boys, on landing in Cape Town, **visited h**im in his cage on the cargo side.

CHAPTER 6

RETURNING HOME
AND A NEW LIFE

On our return from London, we bought a house in Fernwood, just opposite the Parliamentary Club. Aside from having certain disadvantages, it turned out to be too far for the boys to cycle to school (Bishops) in Rondebosch. So, Anita and I then bought a more spacious house in Rondebosch, in which we lived until the boys finished school and university and left home.

It was also home to Woden – probably one of the most well-travelled dogs in the world, having been born in Australia, adopted by a diplomatic family in that country, lived in ambassadorial splendour in London and finally settled in an attractive family home with spacious grounds in the fine suburb of Rondebosch, Cape Town, where he was mated with a dog called Gotcha, who had a litter of six pups, one of which we retained (or Lyndon did), calling him Runty because of his puny size. (Like Jock of *Jock of Bushveld* fame, he was smallest of the litter.)

Runty was an extremely energetic and lively dog, which was also his undoing. One night, quite late, after a party the boys had held, Runty slipped out of the front gate and was fatally hit by a car. I remember holding him on the ground and suggesting to Lyndon he feel his heart beating which, sadly, was to no avail.

Shortly after this Woden, who was painfully showing his age, had to be put down and that sad task was left to me to arrange. That left Gotcha and Oscar, whom we had acquired by this time, and Anita and me, in this large family home, and so we decided to sell it and move on to something more compact, which we found in the adjoining suburb of Newlands.

A DOG HAS DIED

BY PABLO NERUDO – A FAMOUS CHILEAN POET WHO ALSO WROTE IN SPANISH

My dog has died.
I buried him in the garden
next to a rusted old machine.
Some day I'll join him right there,
but now he's gone with his shaggy coat,
his bad manners and his cold nose,
and I, the materialist, who never believed
in any promised heaven in the sky
for any human being,
I believe in a heaven I'll never enter.
Yes, I believe in a heaven for all dogdom
where my dog waits for my arrival
waving his fan-like tail in friendship.

Ai, I'll not speak of sadness here on earth,
of having lost a companion
who was never servile.
His friendship for me, like that of a porcupine
withholding its authority,
was the friendship of a star, aloof,
with no more intimacy than was called for,
with no exaggerations:
he never climbed all over my clothes
filling me full of his hair or his mange,
he never rubbed up against my knee
like other dogs obsessed with sex.

No, my dog used to gaze at me,
paying me the attention I need,
the attention required
to make a vain person like me understand
that, being a dog, he was wasting time,
but, with those eyes so much purer than mine,
he'd keep on gazing at me
with a look that reserved for me alone
all his sweet and shaggy life,
always near me, never troubling me,
and asking nothing.

(continued...)

Ai, how many times have I envied his tail
as we walked together on the shores of the sea
in the lonely winter of Isla Negra
where the wintering birds filled the sky
and my hairy dog was jumping about
full of the voltage of the sea's movement:
my wandering dog, sniffing away
with his golden tail held high,
face to face with the ocean's spray.

Joyful, joyful, joyful,
as only dogs know how to be happy
with only the autonomy
of their shameless spirit.
There are no good-byes for my dog who has died,
and we don't now and never did lie to each other.

So now he's gone and I buried him,
and that's all there is to it.

OUR NEW HOME

Twenty years ago we bought our present home in Newlands, Cape Town. It was and is called Montrose House and is the oldest house, having been built in 1851. It originally was a farmhouse, with the surrounding land carrying cows and horses and market gardens, which would gradually be overtaken by houses and blocks of apartments and of course, about 20 years ago, the gated complex of four houses and an open square providing access to the houses and their garages called Montrose Terrace. There are electronically operated pedestrian and vehicular gates leading to the street. It is an arrangement that encourages the best of neighbourly relations, offers space for children and pets, while at the same time quite naturally ensuring a high level of security. What is common to the four houses is that they have small walled-off gardens, three of them with compact swimming pools. As regards our own house, the main wall boards onto the street with the side wall right next to the electronic gates and specifically the engraved names of the houses, their numbers and buttons for callers, whether expected visitors or delivery people, to announce their presence.

With our furnishings and enough books to fill the walls of no less than three rooms, we also brought from Rondebosch to Newlands the two dogs – Gotcha and Oscar – expecting them to settle in as well as they did in the Rondebosch house. But it was not to be. Their inability to see beyond those walls and the lack of human companionship (Anita and I both worked away from home at the time) set them barking non-stop, causing complaints to pour in from Montebello, the big block of flats across the street.

Obviously, something drastic needed to be done. Gotcha, of whom Anita and I were particularly fond, (she had produced a litter in our Rondebosch house), was very old and partially solved the problem when she passed on shortly after the move. When our son Chris chose to adopt Oscar, Anita and I became dogless for the first time in our marriage, since first accidentally acquiring Mandy in 1970, and we would remain so until the 31st of January 2017, when we brought home a puppy we called Posh.

CHAPTER 7

THE DOG STORY: WHAT I KNEW AND WHAT I HAVE LEARNT

What should be clear is that there has not been a single pure-bred dog in my and my family's life. (By the way, according to Hills, the international pet food company, there are now around 360 officially recognised dog breeds in the world!) As far as our personal canine family is concerned, the closest to being pure bred was probably Mandy (a boxer). From what my favourite vet tells me, mongrels as opposed to pure breds are much more resilient to ailments and disease. And in any event, being a mongrel doesn't make a dog any less lovable. Jess, mother of Jock, was one.

Incidentally, another fact about our family's dogs is that, with the exception of Runty who was born in our house in Rondebosch, all our dogs have come to us as adoptees from dog homes or as dog refugees – off the street so to speak – something more recently made popular by French President Emmanuel Macron, American President Joe Biden and British Prime Minister Boris Johnson. Of the three dogs, Prime Minister Johnson's pet, who is called Dilyn, appeared quickly to achieve some degree of fame because of a general lack of discipline and a fondness for chewing the antiques at **No 10 Downing**

Street, which is of course the Prime Minister's official residence.

Dilyn, who is a Jack Russell-cross, was reported by *The London Times* "for also leaving little gifts in the grounds of Buckingham Palace where Prime Minister Johnson is allowed to exercise with him". One reporter said that the PM isn't good at remembering to clean up after his "slack-bowelled" friend. Fortunately, apparently watchful gardeners keep a supply of plastic bags at hand.

Although not directly relevant, the point should be made that dogs often feature in politics. President Charles de Gaulle is known to have said: "The better I get to know men, the more I find myself loving dogs". And President Barack Obama significantly said of himself: "A lot of shelter dogs are mutts like me!"

THE NEW DOG

BY LINDA PASTAN, AN AMERICAN POET AND POET **LAUREA**TE OF MARYLAND

Into the gravity of my life,
the serious ceremonies
of polish and paper
and pen, has come
this manic animal
whose innocent disruptions
make nonsense
of my old simplicities–
as if I needed him
to prove again that after
all the careful planning,
anything can happen.

CHAPTER 8

WE ADOPT A PUPPY

From about 2015, I began increasingly working from home with my study being converted into an office. About this time, I also began writing my memoir, which was published in 2018. Anita, however, continued as full-time director of Pro Ed School and Centre.

One day at the end of January 2017 I received a phone call from Anita's secretary, asking me to come and fetch a puppy. I didn't know what she was talking about, but nonetheless did what I was expected to do, returning home with an attractive little black female puppy of no obvious breed which, once in the house, took off and spent the rest of the day hiding behind the piano stool.

The explanation was that Anja Nolte, one of the teachers at Pro Ed, **and her husband Cobus, who were dog-lovers, had adopted a dog off the streets of** Heideveld in 2015. It had been brought to Anja by one of the assistants at the school who lived in that large township. In mentioning this later in a group where Anita was present, Anita had apparently said she was interested in getting a dog. That was in 2015.

Two years later Patricia, the same assistant, told Anja of another similar situation where an obviously homeless dog was at her door every morning looking for food. Patricia said her circumstances were such that she could not continue doing this and she could not take the dog in. Anja asked her not to return the dog to the streets but to hold it and that same afternoon after work she took Patricia home, fetched the puppy and took her directly to the Tygerberg Animal Hospital. On the way she phoned Anita and told her about the dog and that she was taking her to the vet. As Anja said: "Anita told me to get done whatever I needed to do to help the dog. She would pay all the expenses."

The vet estimated that the dog was between five and six months old and, after having been examined, she had her first injection, was de-wormed and had a blood sample taken to be sure there was nothing we needed to worry about. According to Anja she was in the clear, although covered in fleas and ticks. The vet gave her a tablet to give to the dog when they got home. When her husband Cobus returned they gave her a thorough bath.

It is a measure of the dogs pathetic circumstances as a wandering street dog that it found the lawn, which she was then free to play on with Anja's dogs, strangely fascinating. We later established from our preferred vet that she was of the *Africanis* breed with a strong Labrador strain.

THE PUPPY IS NAMED POSH

The next day Anja took the dog with her to school, where it seems she played with and delighted Anja's class until 10 o'clock, when Anita was free to see her and the puppy in what was a rather joyfully emotional meeting in her office. It was at that point that Anita apparently called the dog Posh because, as she explained later, of her white chest, white feet and white-tipped tail against a generally black body; call it the tuxedo effect. And it is at that point that I was instructed to come and fetch a puppy!

I think it is evident from the above that I personally have recollections of all the dogs in our family down the years. I am sure that in many instances I would have greatly benefited at this point had I been able to share my memories with my parents and particularly my mother and my two brothers, but regrettably they've all passed on and with them their memories of our dogs.

CHAPTER 9

A DIFFERENT DOG EXPERIENCE

My experience with Posh was clearly different from with any other dog. According to Anja's calculations, Posh was born around the 25th of August 2016 and we took possession of her on the 31st of January 2017 when she was therefore five months old. From that point on my, and to a considerable extent **Anita's experience with Posh has been very close.**

As I dictate this, she lies stretched out on a carpet in front of my desk. I don't just see her briefly in the morning, before I go to an office, and in the evening when I return home. I see her regularly during the day and am reminded of her existence when somebody rings a bell at the complex's gate or somebody walks a dog past the gate or one of the ever-friendly neighbours picks up one of the tennis balls and throws it for Posh to fetch. Or at around 5 o'clock, when she stands in the study doorway silently staring at me, I know that if she could talk she would be saying: "Buddy, it is time for our evening walk with supper to follow!"

One important variation to this schedule has been the involvement of my secretary Debbie. She began working as my secretary in the various businesses I was involved in 2013. And, as these fell away, she took over as private secretary managing appointments and assisting with publications and so on. For example, she put together the footnotes for my memoir *The Independent Factor* and liaised with the distributor.

With two sons and their families in London, Anita and I did a fair amount of travel (regrettably curtailed by Covid) and Debbie would act as caretaker and look after the house and Posh, with whom she has developed a very close relationship. Taking her for her morning walk is now one of her duties and something Posh keenly anticipates.

POSH'S NEW HOME

Our home is on two floors with most of the living area downstairs, the main bedroom and a large study/television room upstairs. Posh has a round, custom-designed bed both downstairs and upstairs. Dogs, as we all know, sleep an average of 12 to 14 hours a day, much of this in the daytime, and when Posh sleeps in the day she sleeps (depending on the weather) either on the veranda (under the window of my study), in the quad itself or (especially when I'm working there) on her bed in my study.

She receives the first meal of the day at around 8:30am **which is followed by a** strenuous walk with Debbie mid-morning, and some ball-fetching in the early afternoon with me. A second walk and some ball-fetching with me is associated with her second meal at about 5:30pm.

THE DOG

BY OGDEN NASH - AMERICAN COMIC POET

The truth I do not stretch or shove
When I state that the dog is full of love.
I've also found by actual test,
A wet dog is the lovingest.

When Anita and I finish dinner, we go upstairs to read and watch television. As for Posh, who will be sitting on a carpet close to the table or under the table, this moment is signified as **"bone time" when she will come upstairs where there are bones which she will chew until she is ready for bed.**

However, most evenings I go up after Anita and it is interesting that Posh never goes before me. Sometimes, she will lie at the bottom of the stairs waiting twenty minutes or so and then go up with me. When she is ready for bed, she has a delightful habit of nudging Anita and me in turn in our easy chairs watching TV (clearly her way of saying good night) and, once acknowledged, then climbing into her basket. At about 8 o'clock the next morning she will quietly come into our bedroom and lie down without disturbing us.

THE MORNING ROUTINE

She will only go downstairs when I go, which is generally after Anita. She will wait at the top of the stairs for me to come and sit next to her and engage in a sort of wrestling game in which I try to get my arm around her chest and pull her down one step and she resists and not so tenderly bites my arm. Getting my arm around her and pulling her down a step appears to end the game. We will then proceed down the stairs with her heading for the front door, knowing that I am likely to open it to fetch the newspapers. She will expect Debbie to come between 10 and 11 o'clock for the morning walk of the day. Obviously, these are all approximations but they indicate a pattern or routine, something that is important in the life of dogs and I suppose to all of us.

Dogs, and their differences and behaviour are of tremendous social interest and frequently

the source of general and dinner-table discussions. And, although I want to stress that I am

nothing of an expert, having developed the interest, read and consulted widely and

followed this up with Posh, what I have learnt I think is worth passing on.

LITTLE DOG'S RHAPSODY INTO THE NIGHT

BY MARY OLIVER, PULITZER PRIZEWINNER

He puts his cheek against mine
and makes small, expressive sounds.
And when I'm awake, or awake enough
he turns upside down, his four paws
in the air and his eyes dark and fervent.
"Tell me you love me," he says.
"Tell me again."
Could there be a sweeter arrangement?
Over and over he gets to ask. I get to tell.

WHAT I KNEW BEFORE POSH CAME INTO OUR LIVES

I did know things like dogs are the oldest domesticated animal, but I subsequently learned that dogs have been in the company of man from probably 10 000 years ago, having originated most likely somewhere in Eurasia 12 000 to 14 000 years ago. And yes, dogs are members of the same family as wolves, jackals and foxes. As such, there are certain features that suit them admirably for a life of hunting: powerful jaws with teeth adapted to seizing prey, keen senses of smell and hearing, and a social instinct that maintains and coordinates the efforts of the pack – a concept it seems of some importance and to which I will return.

I have also come to appreciate (because this is something that is pretty obvious) that the dog is a highly social animal, whose original well-being and normal psychological development are products of association with other dogs in a pack. According to my sources, the dog in its past evolution was less wary of humans than was the wolf and adventured more boldly into human past settlements to feed. And humans in turn may have grown to depend on the dog to warn of approaching threats, with the dog in turn beginning to depend on humans for food and shelter.

Mutual bonds of benefit and affection probably strengthened gradually over the centuries until, through breeding and the selection of traits and appearances, the most domestic dog became man's creation.

CHAPTER 10

THE DOMESTICATED DOG

The domesticated dog apparently spread very rapidly all over the world, through both hemispheres and from tropical to arctic climates. When the Europeans arrived in North America, they brought their own dogs with them, but every Indian tribe already had them. At that time there were at least 20 distinct breeds in North and South America. Most of these have disappeared except for the Mexican hairless and the Eskimo dogs.

In Australia there is the dingo, a species separate from the domestic dog. Typically a wild animal, the dingo is sometimes found semi-domesticated in Aboriginal settlements. Its ancestors must've been brought as domestic dogs to Australia by the first immigrants several thousand years ago and later allowed to run wild.

Since the beginning of history, dogs have been found all over Africa. Other varieties of dogs lived throughout Asia and on most of the oceanic islands. According to my sources, most is known about the history of European dogs. From the earliest times, traders and travellers not only took their favourite dogs on long journeys but often returned with new and exotic varieties. Dogs were in no way all cultivated then in England. In fact, when John Caius (the founder of Caius College of Cambridge University) wrote a description of English dogs, he listed six main varieties of dogs – Greyhounds, Hounds, Pointing dogs, sometimes called bird dogs, Terriers, Mastiffs, and Shepherd dogs. A basic group of dogs not mentioned by Caius includes the sled dogs of the Eskimo, found in the Artic in both America and Eurasia.

THE MAIN GROUPS OF DOMESTIC DOGS

Because of differences in how they define them, there is no complete agreement among dog experts on how many groups of domestic dogs there are, but there's no disagreement among them that the DNA and even basic skeletal structures remain identical to that of the wolf. However, depending on the purposes for which they were bred, several hundred different breeds of dog now exist in every conceivable shape, size and design, fitting into seven main groups. Following the English expert Jan Fennell, these include:

Gundogs or Sporting Dogs

This group quite clearly evolved according to the jobs humans need them to do. For example, dogs with sensitive noses were bred to locate or "point" to the hunter's targets; other breeds were developed to flush out or "spring" the prey, usually birds.

And then there were dogs trained to "retrieve", which were bred specifically with "soft" mouths so as not to hurt the prey on retrieving it. A few examples of the breeds are Golden Retrievers, the Shorthaired Pointer, the Irish, Gordon and English Setters and the Labrador Retrievers.

Working Dogs

Over the centuries, humans have trained dogs to do a wide range of different jobs. They are being produced specifically to rescue people from drowning, guide them across snow-covered mountains, alert them to intruders, sniff out drugs and similar jobs. The wide collection of specific breeds includes the Alaskan Malamute, St Bernard, the Dobermann and the Boxer, as examples. These search and rescue dogs aid in earthquakes, for example the Fridain Mexican earthquake, and avalanches.

Hounds

Some of the earliest breeds developed by man were used as "sight" or "gaze" hounds. Their special skill was to hunt down prey that humans and their horses, bows and arrows couldn't reach in open country. These dogs have the ability to creep up swiftly and silently, running down the prey so that the hunters could close in for the kill.

This need produced one of the greatest contrasts within the canine world – from the tallest of breeds, the Irish Wolfhound, to the Dachshund, one of the shortest, and the Greyhound, one of the fastest.

Terriers

Terriers were bred to hunt perceived vermin both above and below the ground, animals such as foxes, badgers, rats and otters. Popular breeds include the Airedale Terrier, the Bullterrier, and the Fox and Irish Terriers.

Toy Dogs

Dogs have not just been bred for working purposes. Throughout history man has used dogs that have provided him with nothing more than warmth and companionship, affection and aesthetic pleasure. Lapdogs, for instance, were – as their name suggests – made specifically to sit on the laps of Tibetan monks. Toy breeds include the Maltese and the Pomeranian, the Pekinese and the Yorkshire Terrier.

Utility or Non-Sporting Dogs

The range of bred dogs is enormous and not surprisingly there are those that do not fall in the main categories of sport or work. These include the Japanese Akita, the miniature Poodle and the Chow Chow.

Pastoral or Herding Dogs

Among the most useful and intelligent dogs ever bred are those traditionally used for herding. They've been trained to work in different climates and with different animals from cattle and sheep to reindeer. The most popular breeds of this type are the German Shepherd, the Border Collie, the old English Sheepdog and the Australian Shepherd, Cattle dogs and others.

DOG INTO THE FUTURE

BY STEPHEN KELEN, A LEADING AUSTRALIAN POET

Through a break in the fence, laneway and away.
To a park or vacant lot. The dog of the city's luck
Proud of his sleekness, blackness. His coat shines, tail
Points to the sky whence he came. Has a mind & memory
though they don't bother him much. The past compressed
into yesterday, tonight is the future. First things first.
There's a smell in the air. Getting stronger.
Goodbye memory! Up there before the alley turns: a corner
A dog party drunk on a smell.
The dog of the city's luck, of fine coat and tail
Known in different streets by different names
But is a true black dog who sends alleys of cats
Screaming home, chases motorbikes, appears when
you're least expecting – one of life's true mystics
and follows people into the local cementary
to see a bone buried but dogs don't get buried.
They disappear before it happens and reappear
When you think they're gone.

CHAPTER 11

THE WOLF IN YOUR PUPPY

There are, not surprisingly given the global interest in dogs, an amazing number of books on dogs, their natures, up-bringing, particular aptitudes and training, and the like, of which I have read or consulted a few. That catchy heading above comes from Jan Fennell's *The Puppy Listener*, which I think is excellent, and refers to a passage which directly follows on her discussion of groups of dogs. In fact, having identified and described the seven groups she writes: "Whatever breed they are – and whatever life they lead – two things are certain. They all share the same DNA and the same basic programming as their ancient ancestor, the wolf. And because of this each of their lives will conform to a distinct pattern. It may not seem as though your adorable ball of fluff is a wild animal as it curls itself up in front of your fireplace but, deep within its DNA, that's precisely what it is."

Fascinating, don't you think? Fennell then goes on to explain in some detail how over the first six months of its life the puppy's life changes. And she tells you how you can facilitate some of those changes or, more accurately, developments. Among the more important are teaching the dog recognition of its name and toilet training.

HOW TO NAME A PUPPY

Once you've chosen the name, you start addressing the puppy within its litter, using that name. At this point the dog doesn't see itself as an individual so much as a member of the litter, so it is possible it will not respond immediately. But if it does, you should get it to stop, look at you and – for the first time – ask "Are you talking to me?" Fennell says there are some key points to remember when doing this:

*Eye contact is crucial. When you call one of the puppies, they may all look at you but you must only look at the individual you are addressing.

*Make sure your eyes are soft and inviting; don't glare or look anxious.

*When you call the name, do so in a happy way; the tone should be soft, as should the body language.

*If the dog comes to you on its own, praise it warmly, repeating the name.

*If the whole litter comes, make a point of only praising the one dog; you are also trying to teach the pups that it is not their name, and this will help reinforce that message. The beauty of this is that it is something you can build on. When you're teaching the dog to make a positive association with something during toilet training, for instance, repeating the name warmly as you reward it will help.

HOW TO TOILET TRAIN A PUPPY

Toilet training: This clearly is a priority matter, and understandably so, to potential dog-owners, which also explains the very considerable literature devoted to the subject; and I must say that Jan Fennell also makes sense on this issue. Initially, the mother takes care of the puppies until generally around the third week when they will begin to defecate and urinate on their own.

This new independence coincides with the mother's gradual removal of herself from the scene. At this stage, a puppy may be expected to urinate 12 or more times a day and will open its bowels 5 to 6 times a day. As Fennell says, dogs are by nature clean creatures so the puppy will try to put as much distance as it can between its sleeping and feeding area and its toilet area. So, the dog-owner should provide in effect a toilet area by laying down some newspapers or absorbent padding. The dog is not going to go there every time, but it will eventually. And a path of newspapers should be laid from an exiting door closest to the "toilet" itself.

Their bowel movement is more active after mealtimes and taking the pup to the desired destination of defecation after mealtimes usually has a successful outcome. Repetition is important, as is your tone and body language when rewarding the correct behaviour. And something that is important and initially impressed me about Posh is how she (and it seems many dogs) want to do their toileting in a natural location. Admittedly, she is no longer a puppy but even when she came to us I seem to recall only three or four occasions when she offloaded in the house and then in a particular spot which is near to an access door to the garden, which was closed at the time. She has never to my knowledge defecated in the central quad to which she has access all day. Regularity, punctuality, timing and consistency are critical factors, as are certain attractive circumstances where she can leave her smell: bushes and hedges, grass patches, and so on.

DOG COMMANDS AND HANDSIGNALS

In addition to teaching a dog its name, you'll find several experts recommending lists of commands. While these are obviously spoken commands, dogs don't understand the words that we use. They respond to certain sounds that they pick up out of the ambient noise.

But, as you will know from your own dog, they are incredibly good at reading body language and distinguishing physical gestures. Hence the importance of hand-signals associated with specific voice commands:

*Come! – Hand diagonally across the chest.

*Stay! – Open hand palm forward

*Sit! – Open hand palm up

*Lie down! – Open hand palm up

*Wait! – Open hand palm forward

*Watch me! – One finger pointed to eye

*Posh! – Mentioning her name in a firm voice, she stops and waits for her next command

These are specifically commands but most dogs, if they are talked to, pick up the meaning of various words. Posh, for example, responds to "walkies", "where is the ball?", "fetch the ball", "wait" and "go". And a critical point that has been made several times is that dogs are very good at detecting emotion in human speech.

DHARMA

BY BILLY COLLINS APPOINTED
US POET LAUREATE IN 2001

The way the dog trots out the front door
every morning
without a hat or an umbrella,
without any money
or the keys to her doghouse

---

never fails to fill the saucer of my heart
with milky admiration.

Who provides a finer example
of a life without encumbrance—
Thoreau in his curtainless hut
with a single plate, a single spoon?
Gandhi with his staff and his holy diapers?

Off she goes into the material world
with nothing but her brown coat
and her modest blue collar,
following only her wet nose,
the twin portals of her steady breathing,
followed only by the plume of her tail.

If only she did not shove the cat aside
every morning
and eat all his food
what a model of self-containment she
would be,
what a paragon of earthly detachment.
If only she were not so eager
for a rub behind the ears,
so acrobatic in her welcomes,
if only I were not her god.

CHAPTER 12

DOGS' ASSOCIATIONS WITH HUMANS

The dog figures prominently in many tales of courage and selfless devotion in the service of humans, of steadfastness and perseverance, of attentiveness and seeming concern for its master or mistress. A most recent instance widely reported on Canadian television is of an elderly man who, caught in a massive snowstorm, had abandoned his car not far from his home but was found dead two days later with his faithful dog alive and well, lying across his chest to keep him warm.

And *The Washington Post* reported recently that a dog adopted from an animal shelter had been credited with saving its new owner after he had a stroke. Brian Myers, who is retired and lives alone, is said to have had a special bond with a German Alsatian named Sadie, **who slept at the foot of his bed. In late January he suffered a** stroke and the dog began licking his face. As he said, **"She could tell that I was in trouble." He grasped her collar and she dragged him to his phone to call for an ambulance. Myers' doctor credited the dog with having saved his life, according to** *The Post*.

Dogs are gregarious, aggressive, and obedient to please man. Wolves are shy, highly intelligent, have an inbred fear of man and are psychologically and sociologically very different from dogs. Incidentally, a book that I found fascinating is called The *Philosopher And The Wolf* by Mark Rowlands, a professor of philosophy at Miami University. He tells a story of how he lived with his dogs and a wolf called Brenin for more than a decade. It is a fascinating story.

DOGS APPRECIATED FOR COMPANIONSHIP

"Novels about dogs" on the web lists dozens of authors and their books, which reflect the many special tasks – hunting, guarding, herding, drafting, sniffing, guiding (for the blind) – that dogs are trained for. In fact, because the close social relationship between dogs and humans appear to many to be similar to the human parent-child relationship, dogs have been used to test various theories of child training. But most popular dogs are brought up and trained to be household pets, appreciated for their companionship, something that to my mind – especially the companionship aspect – is poignantly captured by Sir Percy FitzPatrick in the following passage from *Jock of The Bushveld*. Remember the context is the gold-diggers and transporters in the Transvaal in the late 19th century.

> *"Go out among them, ever moving on, whose white bones mark the way for others feet – who shun the cities, living in the wilds and move in silence, self-contained. Who knows what they think, or dream, or hope, or suffer? Who can know? For speech among that hard-schooled lot is but a half-*

remembered art. Yet something you may guess, since with the man there often goes – his dog; his silent tribute to The Book. Oh, it is little they know of life who cannot guess the secret springs of loneliness and love that prompt the keeping of a trifling pet; who do not know what moves a man who daily takes his chances of life and death – man whose breath is in his nostrils – to lay his cheek against the muzzle of his comrade dog, and in trackless miles of wilderness feel he has a friend. Something to hold to; something to protect."

DOG COMPANIONSHIP AS WE GET OLDER

As the more elderly dog-lovers reading this will immediately acknowledge, the companionship their pet provides is increasingly important to the life they lead. This is not difficult to imagine –age restricts movement, emigration takes children and grandchildren to far-off places that are physically unreachable in times of Covid 19 anguish, modern-day communication technology becomes more expensive and complicated for the elderly and regular bridge partners fall by the wayside. My wife and I, now in our eighties, are naturally aware of these – shall we call them challenges? – and have **thoughts as** to how they can be managed with the help of our devoted canine pets.

"A dog is the only thing on earth that loves you more than he loves himself." Josh Billings, the author of books on dogs.

"Dogs are not our whole life, but they make our lives whole." – Roger Caras, the American poet, writer and *wildlife photographer.*

And the widely quoted observation of Konrad Lorenz, 1973 Nobel Prize winner in physiology: "The bond with a dog is as lasting as the ties on this earth could ever be."

CHAPTER 13

TO BE MORE SPECIFIC ABOUT THE PSYCHOLOGY OF DOGS

A frequently-made observation in books about dogs is that we humans generally interpret dog behaviour in terms of our own psychology. So, we think that dogs are just like us. In other words, we humanise our dogs by attributing human emotions to them. At a trivial level, people do this when, for example, they arrange birthday parties for their dogs or when they talk to them as they would to a child. As the American dog behaviourist Cesar Millan, in his *Short Guide to a Happy Dog,* says: "Because we're constantly explaining dog problems in human terms, our relationships with our dogs suffer. What we fail to see time and again is that the solution we use for a human is totally wrong for solving a dog's problems.

Dog psychology, he says, is very different from human psychology. Rather than examining human emotion and reactions, dog psychology tries to understand and explain dog behaviour from a *canine's* perspective rather than from a human one. And that means *"you must understand who dogs are and what they need as dogs in their natural state"*. Which at the core are results of thousands of years of evolution as wild dogs. These powerful forces, says

Millan, are fundamental truths that must be understood by dog owners to live in harmony with dogs.

CESAR MILLAN'S FIVE FUNDAMENTAL TRUTHS ABOUT DOGS.

Firstly, dogs are instinctual. Humans are intellectual, emotional and spiritual. To understand our dogs, we must always remember this,

Secondly, energy is everything as far as dogs are concerned. A dog's mind works by watching our body postures and getting information about the environment through its senses – primarily smell, then sight and sound.

Millan makes the significant point that, if a dog can detect bombs, drugs and lost humans, that same dog should be an expert in understanding and sensing our moods, emotions and energy, which I certainly believe is true of Posh.

Thirdly, dogs are first animals, then species, then breed and then name. Millan acknowledges that there are differences in the intelligence and trends of various breeds, and there are also a lot of individual variations among dogs of the same breed. But breed alone doesn't explain how dogs behave or how "trainable" they are.

Fourthly, a dog's senses form its reality. Humans experience the world primarily through sight; we see a colourful, vibrant world. But dogs see the world primarily through smell, followed by sight in shades of grey, like watching black-and-white TV. Millan says: "Because the sensory experiences of humans and canines are so distinct from each other, how could a dog and human ever experience the same world?"

What we *see,* we experience, what a dog smells it experiences. Humans see each other first and begin to form opinions and likes based on what they see. Dogs smell a human, usually from distances greater than 50 yards away, and begin to develop an understanding of who that person is based on smell.

This difference when ignored results in the irrationality of humans when they see a new dog for the first time leaning down to try and pat it. Humans do this because touch is their second strongest sense. But if dogs could talk, they would be saying: "Human, get out of my face, I don't know you yet."

A DOG'S SOUL

AUTHOR UNKNOWN

Every dog must have a soul, somewhere deep inside
Where all his hurts and grievances are buried with his pride.

Where he decides the good and bad, the wrong way from the right,
And where his judgement carefully is hidden from our sight.

A dog must have a secret place, where every thought abides,
A sort of close acquaintance that he trusts in and confides.

And when accused unjustly for himself, He cannot speak,
Rebuked, He finds within his soul, the comfort he must seek.

He'll love, tho'he is unloved, and he'll serve tho'badly used,
And one kind word will wipe away the times when he's abused.

Altho' his heart may break in two, his love will still be whole,
Because God gave to every dog an understanding Soul!

CHAPTER 14

A DOG'S SENSES

The two senses most supremely developed in the dog are hearing and, pre-eminently, smell. The dog's world is primarily one of scents, as man's is one of sights. The dog's nasal passages are so arranged that a greater volume of air can be drawn over the sensitive lining than is the case with humans. Rapid sniffs carry messages to the enlarged olfactory centre in the brain where the scents are analysed and catalogued. Practical scents seem to be of the greatest interest – the scents that identify other animals: blood, sweat, excrement, urine and smells associated with the sex organs. Grassy smells, soil and ripe, putrefactive odours are likewise attractive.

Our experience with Posh bears this out. When she has her walk around the neighbourhood or in parks, she dawdles and sniffs trees and the ground, trying to pick up food, other dog's scents, old bones, pieces of bread and similar smells.

On the weekly refuse collection days, Posh dawdles much longer during her walk to smell just about every bin in the hopes of finding something that to her is tasty!

HEARING

Hearing is an acute sense in the dog; frequencies of up to 35 000 vibrations per second can be detected, compared with 25 000 in the cat and 20 000 in humans. A Labrador's **hearing is** quite extraordinary! They are often used as service dogs because of their keen ears. As soon as Debbie arrives in the morning and parks her car across the road, Posh immediately hears her and yelps continuously with excitement until she takes her out for a walk.

VISION

On the other hand, sight is a relatively poorly developed faculty in the dog compared to their other senses – although sight at night is better than ours. Moving forms are readily discerned but a still object with no particular odour may go unnoticed. The dog is colour-blind (even guide dogs, which respond to traffic signals, do so by the position of the lighted signal rather than by the colour). On a walk, Posh's direction can change in an instant when she spots birds or squirrels and she thoroughly enjoys chasing them until they are out of danger. She can spot a dog being walked by their owner instantly and, if she is not on her leash, darts to them to in effect say hello.

DOG BEHAVIOUR

The Wolf-Dog pattern. Many aspects of dog behaviour can only be understood with reference to the lives of their wild ancestors, the wolves. In recent years, the behaviour of wolves in undisturbed wild conditions has been studied scientifically, reducing much of the mythology surrounding them to scientific fact. Jan Fennell's statement, which I quoted earlier in the chapter *The wolf in your puppy*, continues to apply, namely: "All dogs, whatever their breed, all share two things: the same DNA and the same basic programming as their ancient ancestor, the wolf. And because of this, each of their lives will conform to a distinct pattern."

Territory and range. Dogs recognise a central headquarters, or a den, that, with the immediate area surrounding it, is defended as a territory from which other dogs are excluded. At various points beyond the central territory dogs will establish "scent posts", with a stop to urinate and defecate.

Males lift the leg to urinate and scratch the ground after defecation. Strange dogs passing by will also mark the place in the same manner. These wolf-like habits are seen especially in dogs allowed to run loose in town or country: the tendency is to defend the immediate areas around the house of the owners, but to wander much more widely, marking certain "scent posts" as they go.

Group activities. A wolf is a highly social animal. Within the pack, wolves are peaceable and very cooperative. While feeding, they observe order, in which the most dominant animal feeds first. Parts of prey animals are often buried, either at the sight of the kill or in the vicinity of the den, presumably to save the food from scavengers. Domestic dogs show the same habits, even attempting to bury such things as dry dog food and bones. Wolves show the same general types of sounds and communication as dogs – barking when a strange animal approaches the den, yelping in fear or distress, growling when threatening another animal, and howling, either alone or, when the pack is together, in unison.

Combative behaviour. Two strange male dogs usually approach each other stiffly, with their tails held erect, and appear to identify each other by sniffing in the tail region. If a fight starts, they rush at each other, snapping and snarling, and the fight will last until one runs away or submits. The beaten animal will roll on its back, extending its paws, yelping and protecting its throat by snapping. The winning animal stands over it, growling and threatening. If dominance has already been established, one dog may indicate this by placing his paw on the other's back and growling while the subordinate animal keeps his tail low. Similar behaviour is seen in wolves.

Courtship and care of young. In courtship, dogs show a characteristic pattern of play. They crouch, extending their forepaws and cocking their heads to one side, then they throw the four legs around each other's necks and wrestle. Males do this to **ascertain** if the bitch is ready to stand and is at her most fertile. This is followed by running and chasing and eventually making love. Like wolves, dogs show the peculiarity of the sexual tie; after copulation, the two animals remain locked together for many minutes. This is needed to allow for enough ejaculation.

CHAPTER 15

PARTICULAR QUALITIES

Intelligence. Judging how intelligent a dog is, either in comparison to other dogs or to other animals, is difficult. Obviously, intelligence is measured primarily by the ease with which a dog can be trained. This may depend in large measure, however, on the degree of motivation in general. When individual dogs are sufficiently motivated there appeared to be no wide differences in intelligence between breeds. There are big differences, however, in the ease with which breeds and individual dogs will accept complex training.

Certain breeds, particularly shepherd dogs and poodles, have reputations for intelligence of this sort. These animals have a high capacity for developing motivation and attention to talk to handlers and a similarly high capacity for accepting inhibitory training.

A highly trained dog is capable of mastering many different commands. The Guinness World Record is 60 tricks in one minute by Sara and her dog Hero on command and Jennifer Fraser and her dog Daiquiri.

At the same time, according to my source, there are definite limitations to canine intelligence. Like other mammals (excluding man), dogs cannot be taught to talk and indeed learn to bark on command only with great difficulty.

There is no evidence that dogs are able to recognise the meaning of words when they are used in new combinations (in other words, to understand new sentences). This means that the amount of information that actually can be conveyed to a dog is quite limited. A well-trained dog, however, is capable of such attentiveness to his owner's slightest movement and mannerisms that it almost seems to read the owner's mind.

CHAPTER 16

INTELLIGENCE ILLUSTRATED

To illustrate the point in terms of Posh, she knows when Anita and I are going out and when she is or is not going with us. She distinctly responds to how we address each other. I embrace Anita and she almost wants to be part of the action: it clearly is something she welcomes. Raised voices have the same effect. She has a very strong temporal sense. In the morning she comes into the bedroom when there has been some movement on our part; and if we are not awake she will quietly lie down.

Around 9:30am, she will indicate in different ways that it is time to go for a walk. It might be by simply making her presence known by staring at me or by bringing a ball to me. And it is very clear, once I have decided that we are going to go for a walk, that she would like Anita to go with us. In fact, when it's not quite clear that Anita is coming and she is around, Posh will agitate at the top of the steps to the house.

Her sense of timing and therefore expectation in the mornings applies to Debbie. She'll wait in the quad near to the gate or on the veranda from about 10:00am. While she responds to every time the entry bell is rung, she is highly agitated when it goes about that time because she senses it is Debbie. She knows all the other neighbours and distinguishes between them and nonresident visitors, at whom she will bark at the main gate. She knows who are regular visitors, like the gardeners and the swimming pool people, and will welcome the char who comes three times a week.

Emotions. Come to think of it, most of a dog's emotional reactions are readily understandable growls and snarls of threat, and barking is usually an alarm signal; rapid horizontal tail wagging indicates a friendly approach and is roughly the social equivalent of the human smile. High-pitched yelping occurs in situations involving pain or terror. The rapid yelps and whines of puppies indicate distress, which may have many causes.

Solitary howling usually indicates loneliness or may be a reply to another howling dog. Some other reactions are less easy to interpret and can be understood only in terms of the behaviour of dogs towards each other. Jumping up and offering the forefeet is usually an attempt to initiate the playful fighting so often seen between dogs. A stiff-legged approach with erect and slowly wagging tail indicates aggressiveness and may be followed by an attack.

A "worried" dog holds his ears down and has his tail between their legs. An attentive dog often displays a wrinkled forehead, usually the result of the erection of the ears. This external expression, however, is not always a true guide to an internal emotional state. A serious prolonged internal emotional disturbance will often show up in depressed activity and loss of appetite.

CHAPTER 17

DOGS AS PETS

Unlike Posh, who was adopted as a pet off the street when she was about five months old, a puppy aged between six and eight weeks is the ideal time to be acquired, in order to permit normal psychological development. The early development of a dog is divided into several distinct periods: Neonatal, Transition, Socialisation and Juvenile.

* In the neonatal (new-born) period the puppy's activity is largely confined to nursing and sleeping. The new-born puppy is blind and deaf and is consequently largely isolated from the external world, as is found with most carnivores.

* In about 14 days its eyes will open, marking the beginning of the transition. During the third week, the puppy undergoes a rapid change in behaviour and in sensory and motor abilities. At the end of the week, when its ears open, the puppy begins to react to sound. At the same time, its first teeth appear, and it will attempt to eat solid food if it is offered. Meanwhile, it has begun to walk instead of crawl and to show social responses to humans and other dogs.

* This marks the beginning of the period of socialisation, at approximately three weeks after birth. The puppy will now slowly approach a strange person, nosing and wagging its tail. Another social response is playful fighting with its littermates.

* At any time during this period, which lasts up to 12 weeks of age, it is easy to form a close social relationship between a puppy and its owner, the maximum favourable response being obtained between six and eight weeks.

* Significantly, by removing a puppy from its litter early in the socialisation period, **all social relationships are transferred to human beings. Emotional disturbance and prolonged yelping** is a normal reaction to removal from the litter and can be relieved by fondling and companionship. The puppy soon associates the owner with relief from distress.

An interesting question, as far as Posh is concerned, is at what stage she made that emotional connection. At the estimated age of five months she was looking for food every morning at people's doors in the expectation of getting something. One wonders what other associations (reliance on humans) of this kind she had before her adoption by Anita and me.

NOW THE CHOICE OF BREED

What breed of dog as a pet? As is evident from discussions with dog owners, everyone has their favourite breed. But vets, dog trainers and breeders qualify their responses with reference to what essentially the dog is required for, for whom it is required, what will be expected of it and the circumstances in which it will live. For example, the age, condition and stage of life of the likely owner is important. Some breeds are more robust than others and require more intensive exercising than is good for an elderly person. Other breeds are placid and can therefore be trusted to have children pull their ears or sit on them.

There is also a question of how much space there is for the dog to play in. For example, is the dog intended for a house or a flat? And most South Africans wanting a dog as a pet like to be assured that it will have at least a modicum of watchdog capability.

"The possession of a dog today is different from the possession of a dog at the turn of the century, when one's dog was fed on mashed potato and brown gravy and lived in the dog house with an arched portal. Today, a dog is fed on scraped beef and Vitamin B1 and lives in bed with you". — EB White.

E.B. White was an extraordinary essayist and satirist, a New Yorker columnist, celebrator of New York City, champion of integrity who during his life in New York owned a dozen dogs.

CHAPTER 18

FASHIONS IN DOGS
BY E.B WHITE

An Airedale, erect beside the chauffeur of a Rolls-Royce,
Often gives you the impression he's there from choice.
In town, the Great Dane is kept by the insane.
Today the Boxer is fashionable and snappy;
But I never saw a Boxer
Who looked thoroughly happy.
The Scotty's a stoic, He's gay and he's mad;
His pace is a snail trot, His harness is plaid.
I once had a bitch, semi-invalid, crazy:
There ne'er was a Scotch girl Quite like Daisy.

Pekes are biological freaks. They have no snout
And their eyes come out. Ladies choose 'm
To clutch to their bosom. A Pekinese would
Gladly fight a wolf or a cougar, but is usually owned
By a Mrs. Applegate Krueger. Cocker are perfect
For Elizabeth Barrett Browning, or to carry
Home a package from the A&P without clowning.

The wire-haired fox, is hard on socks
With or without clocks. The smooth-haired variety
Has practically vanished from nice society,
And it certainly does irk us that you

Never see one except when you go to the circus.
The dachshund's affectionate,
He wants to wed with you:
Lie down to sleep, and he's in bed with you.
Sit in a chair, He's there.
Depart, You break his heart.

My Christmas will be a whole lot wetter and merrier
If somebody sends me a six-weeks-old Boston terrier.
Sealyhams have square sterns and cute faces
Like toy dogs you see at Macy's.
But the Sealyham, while droll in appearance,
Has no clearance.

Chows come in black, and chows come in red;
They could come in bright green, I wouldn't turn my head.
The roof of their mouth is supposed to be blue,
Which is one of those things that might easily be true.
To us it has never seemed exactly pleasant
To see a beautiful setter on East Fifty-seventh Street
looking for a woodcock or a pheasant.

German shepherds are useful for leading the blind,
And for biting burglars and Consolidated Edison men in the
behind.
Lots of people have a rug. Very few have a pug.

CHAPTER 19

SOME WORTHY DOG CHARITIES

At an earlier point in the book, I mentioned that there are estimated to be nine million dogs in South Africa, of which 85% are in townships. Those dogs have a lifespan of between four to six years because most of the inhabitants of those townships don't have access to, or the financial resources to pay for veterinary care. Due to dogs mainly roaming the streets freely, preventable illnesses such as canine distemper or panleukopenia, can spread very quickly. Likewise, many dogs die as a result of rabies, as only 15% of animals are vaccinated regularly against the virus or the animals are killed out of fear of possible infection.

Posh, it will be recalled, was one of those strays who, if it were not that somebody had taken her off the street, by today would be dead. Against that background and the celebration of Posh I decided to include some of the Rescue Centres below, all of whom, with others, against tremendous odds make an important contribution to the health and happiness of South African dogs. And obviously, we ask you to look at supporting them in their efforts. Note that taken together they have a presence in most parts of the country.

National Council of SPCAs. To prevent cruelty and promote the welfare of all animals. Five Societies for the Prevention of Cruelty to Animals have been closed countrywide because of the challenges faced by the NPO.

nspca@nspca.co.za / +27 0 11 907 3590.

Domestic Animal Rescue Group (DARG) Cape Town + 27 0 21 790 0383 / **www.darg.org.za**

Woof Projects, Cape Town. Adoption initiative powered by Oscars Arc – a registered NPO born to inspire *dog* **adoption and save** *dogs'* lives. +27 **0 81 347 0784** / **www.oscarsarc.org**

Dogtown SA Animal Rescue Centre, Gauteng. A shelter only for dogs who have lost their families or have been rescued.

www.dogtownsa.org / **info@dogtownsa.org** / **+27 0 76 044 1979.**

Woodrock Animal Shelter, Pretoria. Rescue, Re-home, Rehabilitate.

www.woodrockanimalrescue.co.za / **+27 0 76 155 4439.**

Animal Anti-Cruelty League (AACL.) South Africa's second largest independent Welfare Organization, relying entirely on the generosity and goodwill of the animal-loving public for financial support. **www.aacl.org.za** / +27 0 11 435 0672.

The BSPCA, Botswana. An NPO that serves to protect all animals against cruelty, to uplift their welfare and that of the communities they live in by educating the public about essential animal care.

www.spca.org.bw / +267 71 820 111

CHAPTER 20

PREFERRED BREEDS: A SHORT LIST OF CANDIDATES AFTER SOME ENQUIRIES

Cocker Spaniels: The family of breeds known as Spaniels dates back at least to the 14th century. By the 19th century there was a group identified as the "cockers" and these were the forebears of today's breed. Cockers have a cheerful and loving temperament and make perfect companions but do tend to bond with one owner. They love water and try to swim in a puddle of mud.

Scottish Terriers: Originally bred to chase the fox and the badger, the Scottie combines strength and bravery. Generally a one-man dog, the terrier is aloof with strangers. The Scottie maintains an air of self-possession and a strong individuality, but it does make a good household pet.

Yorkshire Terriers: Yorkshire Terriers originated in the

mid-19th century, around the industrial heartlands of northern England. They were bred by working men, for whom a large dog would have been difficult to keep, but who wanted a lively companion. Yorkshire Terriers are surprisingly domineering for their size, and very good watchdogs.

WAITING FOR HAPPINESS

BY NOMI STONE, AWARD-WINNING AMERICAN
POET AND A PRINCETON RESEARCH FELLOW

*Dog knows when friend will come home
because each hour friend's smell pales,
air paring down the good smell
with its little diamond. It means I miss you
O I miss you, how hard it is to wait
for my happiness, and how good when
it arrives. Here we are in our bodies,
ripe as avocados, softer, brightening
with latencies like a hot, blue core
of electricity: our ankles knotted to our*

> *calves by a thread, womb sparking*
> *with watermelon seeds we swallowed*
> *as children, the heart again badly hurt,*
> *trying and failing. But it is almost five*
> *says the dog. It is almost five.*

Boxers: A sturdy, energetic dog, always full of high spirits and making an excellent guard dog. The boxer probably has its origins in German dogs of the mastiff type, used for bear-baiting in medieval times. A lively, often boisterous dog, despite its fierce background the boxer is generally trustworthy, but it is important to get puppies from a reputable breeder. Boxers require lots of exercise.

Dachshunds were originally bred to hunt foxes and rabbits as well as badgers, their smaller size allowing them to pursue the animals underground. The original dogs were of standard size, but towards the end of the 19th century smaller dogs were developed. Miniature dogs are the most popular. All dachshunds are very lively, particularly the smooth-haired breed. They also make good watchdogs. A romp in a large garden usually provides enough exercise.

For Dachshund owners.

> I like to read books on dog training. Being the owner of dachshunds, to me a book on dog discipline becomes a volume of inspired humour. Every sentence is a riot! – EB White.

Schnauzer: This jaunty, intelligent little dog has won more admirers than either of the other schnauzers, the Standard and Giant. The breed originated in the cattle and sheep farming areas of southern Germany. Records of a schnauzer-type dog date back to the early 16th century. Schnauzers are full of good-natured energy, and are very friendly with children. Long walks and regular, careful grooming of the coarse coat will be required.

MY HEART BELONGS TO A SCHNAUZER

Author Unknown

My heart belongs to a Schnauzer
Bushy, flowing moustache,
With eyes that pierce your heart
Protective and intelligent – A friend right from the start.
A dog who loves to romp and play, so spirited and fun,
Yet always there to listen
To your cares when day is done.
A charming disposition – Affectionate and sweet
A Schnauzer shares my world each day,
And makes my life complete !

The Pug is a breed of dog with physically distinctive features of a wrinkly, short-muzzled face and a curled tail. The breed has a fine glossy coat that comes in a variety of colours. Temperamentally playful, affectionate, charming, stubborn, clever, quiet and calm, yet sociable.

Labrador Retriever: The Labrador has become one of the best-known companion dogs in the world and the dog most favoured as a guide to the blind. The main reason for the Labrador's success as a pet is its personality: a good-temperament, reliable with children, but not so placid as to fail to defend property. They require a fair amount of exercise and a love of water and swimming is an inescapable part of its past as a fisherman's dog in Newfoundland. They have a love of food and hence have a tendency to be overweight if not exercised enough.

Posh and Friends

CARD OF THANKS

BY E.B. WHITE

A spaniel's ears hang low, hang low;
They mop the sidewalk as they go.
Instead of burrs and beggar's-lice,
They pick up things not half so nice.

Spaniels deserve our special thanks
For mopping floors in shops and banks,
Resourceful, energetic, keen,
They keep the city nice and clean.

Spaniels should be exempt from tax
And be supplied with Johnson's wax.

CHAPTER 21

DOGS AND CHILDREN

I t is of course a long time ago, but I can't think of any problematic situations our children had with our dogs. And as far as Posh is concerned, this is where the Labrador in her nature reflects itself. We've actually seen her overcome reserve if not fear in four of our grandchildren, and she clearly delights in seeing our neighbouring children – three young girls: the eldest is about four and the twins eighteen months old – when they come into the quad.

INFORMATION FOR PARENTS

There are many good reasons for introducing your children to dogs. Dogs help children's self-esteem and assist in teaching responsibility and empathy. Living with a dog has health benefits: studies have shown that those children who are exposed for their first years with dogs have lower risks of developing allergies and asthma as they get older. However, these benefits are not automatic.

Much depends on parents teaching kids acceptable boundaries and rules regarding interaction with the dog. And teaching the dog appropriate behaviour when interacting with children.

Management and proper socialisation are the foundation for a safe and fun environment for both children and dogs. Once again, to the ever-changing world we live in especially during Covid, the dog-child relationship is even more important for some as this is the only direct socialisation they get.

THE PSYCHOLOGICAL EFFECT
OF DOGS ON CHILDREN

This is a subject that has been extensively researched in the United States and there is no reason to assume that these studies are not relevant to countries like South Africa and Australia as well. But in a notable publication in 2008, there is a powerful bond between *people and pets*. The psychologist Elizabeth Anderson wrote: "Nothing less than an alchemy is involved when animals and children get together, and the resulting magic has healing properties that work well." And this is the general conclusion of a more recent and major review of no less than 22 studies of the impact of companion animals have on child development. While some of the findings are mixed, the authors concluded that growing up with pets is linked to higher self-esteem, cognitive development and social skills.

In responding to the question, "What is it about living with pets that makes kids better off?" the authors of the review suggested several possibilities. These include the impact of pets on reducing stress, providing social support and companionship, and improving children's communication skills. Another study showed that children raised in families with pets were reported by their parents to:-

* Have better general health
* Be more obedient
* Be more physically active
* Be less moody
* Have fewer behaviour problems
* Have fewer learning difficulties

A more general response to the question "How does having a dog affect a child?" is:

Feeding and caring for a dog encourage child responsibility. Children with dogs display improved impulse control, social skills and self-esteem. Sharing the love and the care of a family dog forges an additional common bond among siblings. Cuddling appeared to reduce stress, loneliness and anxiety.

CHAPTER 22

WHAT BREED IS BEST AS A CHILD'S PET?

Some General Observations.

* **Size**. Small dogs are not the best choice for a young child. Small dogs are fragile and can easily be hurt by a child pulling its ears or tail. Larger dogs are better able to tolerate the activity, the noise and rough play that is part of a dog's life with children. For teenagers, small animals may be better to teach responsibility.

* **Something about breed**. While the several specialists we consulted all had their favourites (see list below), the fact is there are some breeds you would not consider as pets in a family with small kids. This includes breeds specifically bred for protective behaviour – for example, Rottweilers and Chow Chows. Neither should you consider dogs from a herding breed, for example Collies and Shepherds, because they sometimes actually "herd" or bully children.

* The above are generalisations and there will be exceptions in all breeds. For example, dogs trained as watchdogs may certainly, with the correct socialisation, turn out to be the best dog for your family.

* One further important observation on the health issue is expressed by the Drake University Centre for veterinary care. It seems recent studies in paediatric health have concluded that children who live with dogs as pets during the first year of life actually have a better immune system than those who do not. The researchers believe exposure to dogs may have positively boosted the maturation of the immune system during infancy. In addition, when they did fall ill, they needed a shorter course of antibiotics compared to children who did not live with pets.

CHAPTER 23

DOGS AND SECURITY

With house-breaking the number one crime in South Africa, and with six South African cities making the top 20 list of the "most dangerous cities in the world", home security is obviously a matter of deep concern. Distinct from home burglaries is the increase in farm attacks and attacks on farmers leading to a rise in horrific deaths. In both instances, whether urban break-ins or farm attacks, dogs have come to play an important defensive role. Virtually all dog training schools in urban areas include anti-crime offerings and one response to farm attacks has been the development of attack strains in dog breeds already known for their physical strength, protection instincts, loyalty and courage, breeds like the Bullmastiff, the German Shepherd and the Rottweiler and others listed below.

But one fearsome breed, developed in South Africa itself and recognised internationally and in the US in particular, is called the Boerboel. Its temperament is described as intelligent, obedient, confident, dominant and territorial. Boerboel are banned in Denmark because they are thought to be used for dog-fighting, and in Russia and Ukraine because they are thought to be just too strong.

The Top 10 Best Guard Dogs.

- Bullmastiff. Known for physical strength, protection instincts, courageousness and extreme family loyalty, the Bullmastiff is one of the best guard dog breeds to have.
- Doberman Pinscher
- Rottweiler
- Komondor
- Puli
- Giant Schnauzer
- German Shepherd
- Rhodesian Ridgeback
- Kuvasz
- Staffordshire Terrier

The Best Guard Dogs in South Africa.

- Boerboel
- German Shepherd
- Rottweiler
- American Pitbull
- Giant Schnauzer

Guard Dogs: One Further Comment

Lists should be taken as guides rather than rules, and this certainly applies in the case of dogs as watchdogs. There certainly would be excellent watchdogs among the breeds listed which would also make good pets. Posh, the mutt, proves the point.

She clearly has the temperament, size and energy levels and the pack involvement of her wolf ancestry to be the superb guard dog she is. And that surely must be the case of many of your dogs, whose essentials are not described on that expert list.

THE WOLF-DOG PATTERN, POSH AND SECURITY

Under the heading of Dog Behaviour on **page 85**, I dealt briefly with what is generally referred to as the wolf-dog pattern and specifically Jan Fennell's statement that: "All dogs, whatever their breed, all share two things. The same DNA and the same basic programming as their ancient ancestor, the wolf. And because of this each of their lives will conform to a distinct pattern." I wondered how this could be illustrated until I started studying dogs in the role of watchdogs and specifically looked at Posh's role in this regard.

As I explained earlier, and at the risk of some repetition, our house is one of four in a gated complex with a fairly large open square providing access to four houses and their garages. All four houses have open fronts onto the square. As I said earlier, it is an arrangement which encourages the best of neighbourly relations, safe playing space for children and pets, while at the same time ensuring a high level of security. It is this that I am specifically focusing on.

As regards pets, there was a cat in No 2, but that has died, leaving only Posh of No 4 to range the complex

– and that she certainly does – starting in the early morning when she comes down the stairs directly to the front door, knowing that I will open it to fetch the newspapers. She goes out and in effect does something like an inspection of the square, after which she comes into the house for the first meal of the day (which, it is important to stress, I give her). As she then spends most of the time in the square, she has entered all four houses and is acknowledged by their occupants as they come and go. Most of them setting her tail wagging with fond words or pats.

She clearly has also come to distinguish between strangers to the property and regular visitors. For example, she knows who are relatives and friends and regular service people (like gardeners and swimming pool attendants). Although the main gate to the complex is often left wide open (for example, as the janitor removes the dustbins) Posh has never to my knowledge, alone and voluntarily, left the complex. She does so always accompanied by Anita and me, or with Debbie, and on a leash. And, while she is known to urinate in the flower beds, I am unaware of her ever defecating in the square. She'll wait to be led across the road and up the street which is lined by a thick hedge. In this way, several of the Montebello residents, particularly those who work in the garden, have come to know Posh, offering friendly greetings when they see her and her master.

I believe the situation I have described is explainable in terms of the Wolf-Dog formula. Firstly, to Posh the inhabitants (or most of them) of the complex form a pack; and secondly, to Posh the housing complex at 5 Montrose Street constitutes a den. If this analysis is correct, the complex's security from a house-breaking point of view is greatly increased, which surely means that the Wolf-Dog formula should feature consciously in architectural design and structure.

JUST A DOG

AUTHOR UNKNOWN

From time to time people tell me, 'lighten up, it's just a dog'.
Or, 'that's a lot of money for just a dog'.
They don't understand the distance travelled,
the time spent, or the costs involved for 'just a dog'.
Some of my proudest moments have come about with 'just a dog'.
Many hours have passed and my only company was 'just a dog'.
But I did not once feel slighted.

Some of my saddest moments have been brought about by 'just a dog'.
And in those days of darkness, the gentle touch of 'just a dog' gave me
comfort and reason to overcome the day....
If you, too, think it's 'just a dog', then you will probably understand phrases like
'just a friend', 'just a sunrise', or 'just a promise'.

'Just a dog' brings into my life the very essence of friendship, trust and pure unbridled joy.

'Just a dog' brings out the compassion and patience that makes me a better person.

Because of 'just a dog', I will rise early, take long walks and look longingly to the future.

So, for me and folks like me, it's not 'just a dog' but an embodiment of all the hopes and dreams of the future, the fond memories of the past and the pure joy of the moment.

'Just a dog' brings out what's good in me and diverts my thoughts away from myself and worries of the day.

I hope that someday they can understand that it's not 'just a dog', BUT that dogs give me humanity and keep me from being just a man or a woman.

So, the next time you hear the phrase 'just a dog' - just smile.... BECAUSE they 'Just don't understand'.

CHAPTER 24

DOGS IN APARTMENTS

The following are some tips from Australia for keeping dogs in apartments.

1. Choose your dog wisely because the truth is some breeds are better suited to apartment life than others. For example, you may have your sights set on a Border Collie. But this type of dog would find such confined quarters to be stressful. That doesn't mean that you must go for an effete breed. I have two friends with muscular pugs in Cape Town in apartments, and they are managing very well. **The fact is that dog sizes differ** and it does lead to more exercise and time outside the apartment.

2. You will in the first place of course have made sure from your landlord that having a dog is permissible.

3. Apartments can be bustling places with people – and pets – constantly coming and going. So, obedience classes and social interaction can help your dog to be comfortable in living in such a busy environment.

4. Set aside an emergency "destruction" fund. Even the best-behaved dogs have slipups from time to time.

And if your dog discovers one day that he quite likes the taste of carpet, you are in for a hefty bill.

5. Plan for potty training. House training your dog is a whole different ballgame if you live in an apartment. You can't simply open the back door to let the dog do his business. You may have stairs, elevators and neighbours to contend with. So, establish a scheduled potty routine which will make things run more smoothly.

6. Find ways to exercise. This is obviously quite critical. All dogs have daily exercise needs and if you've a puppy in an apartment you'll need to set aside time every day for leashed walks or hit up the local dog park or consider hiring a dog-walker to help your dog burn off steam.

7. Be a good neighbour and ensure that your dog is vaccinated and is parasite-free. This is especially important when you're sharing outdoor space with children and fellow residents.

8. A relentless barker can cause serious problems between otherwise friendly neighbours. Be courteous, and find ways to curb your dog's yappy vocalisation before the complaints start pouring in. Regular exercise and puzzle toys help in this regard. Devocalisation should be the last resort if continuous barking occurs.

Certain breeds bark more: examples are Jack Russell Terriers, Yorkshire Terriers and Chihuahuas.

9. If your apartment block has a community pool, don't consider it an open invitation for your dog to take a dip. It is not the most sanitary thing to do, and your dog's nails could cause serious damage.

10. If you live in an apartment block where neighbours are just a thin wall away, find a way to block out the extra noise. Play soft, soothing music while you are away to keep your dog calm. A TV or portable fan can have a similar effect. The fewer disturbances your dog hears, the less likely he'll be to sound his barking alarm.

11. Be careful when entering or leaving your apartment. If your dog always reacts to other people or pets, check to make sure the coast is clear before walking through doors. Maintaining a friendly relationship with your neighbour down the hall is easier when you're not startling him every time you come home with your dog.

12. Keep your dog leashed. It might be hard to believe, but not everyone is fond of your Boxer. In fact, there are plenty of people who consider him a threatening menace. So, be sensitive to your fellow neighbours and keep your dog on a leash every time you leave

your apartment. This courtesy extends well beyond your neighbours – it also keeps your dog from getting loose or running into traffic.

CHAPTER 25

DOGS AND VACATIONS

What do you do with your dog when you go on vacation?

* First of all, if you are somebody who simply can't do without your dog when

on vacation, you can ask the location to provide the answer. Consult the website for resorts that welcome pets.

*However, for most people the vacation location is pre-determined. Maybe they make provision for dogs. Again, consult the website.

*However long your vacation, there are three main options for your pet during that period.

You can have someone take care of your pet in your house; secondly, you can have your pet go to someone else's place; or thirdly, you can take your pet with you. What you do with these options depends on how long you are travelling for, how much money you're willing to spend and how much you trust others to take care of your extended family.

*Although dogs might become lonesome, from a pet's point of view there certainly are advantages in being left at home, which is a familiar setting with food, toys, garden and the like are already set up, and your pet knows the lay of the land. There are no other animals to compete or fight with. Your pets can eat the same foods as usual and keep up with the same daily routine. And, depending on the relationship, the person looking after the dog will also maintain a watchful eye over the property.

*To oversee this arrangement, you can ask a neighbour, a friend or a family member who lives nearby. Alternatively, you can get a professional sitter, which of course could involve considerable expense. Professional sitters can be obtained from veterinary clinics, pet shops and dog parlours. If you want to make their job a little easier, you might install an automatic water fountain and food dispenser for your dog.

When Anita and I have spent any time away from the house, Debbie has stepped in, and when we've travelled abroad she has moved into the house. To some extent, this explains the close relationship between her and Posh.

CHAPTER 26

DOGS AND EXERCISE

This is severely limited, due to our ever-changing lifestyle and property sizes. The average dog needs two to three walks per week for exercise and sensory stimulation. Due to Posh's size, her daily routine allows for much of this.

Every dog needs regular exercise to keep fit and healthy. Dogs who don't get enough exercise become obese and lazy. Generally, according to the people I have spoken to, a dog will take as much exercise as you the owner want to take yourself. However, if you are very athletic and enjoy hill-climbing or long-distance jogs, you need to gradually build up this capability in your dog if you want it to accompany you.

I am told that large dogs, particularly giant breeds, should never be over-exercised or overfed before they are 12 months old. Bones and muscles are still developing and too much exercise can cause long-term problems, particularly in joints.

Walking is basic to most dog exercises and there are a number of misunderstandings around it. Most people believe *brisk* walking is essential, something that obviously causes problems for elderly persons who therefore are put off owning a dog or feel they need to engage professional dog-walkers, so losing out on the sheer pleasure of being with their dog and sharing what is a very pleasurable if not essential activity for it. This, however, is a misplaced response. Bear in mind the strength of a dog's sense of smell to a dog's wellbeing – something that a dog running with a jogging master loses out on. Posh on her leash, from the opening of the gate and with a nose that is prickling, starts taking in every invisibly peed-upon plant, every disgusting turd, every discarded food parcel. Then, having chosen precisely where to deposit, after offloading uses both front paws to disturb the foliage, making sure she is leaving her scent for other dogs. One expert likens when your dog finds something delectable – like a cake of fresh warm cow's dung – and decides to role in it so strengthening its own smell, to putting on aftershave!

All too often Posh, when walking with Anita and me, sniffs around for diversions and picks up rubbish. **This is not a problem when Posh walks with Debbie because she is a brisk walker effectively forcing Posh to walk faster.**

And I give Posh regular (three or four times a day) workouts chasing tennis balls – "fetch ball" is one of the phrases she seems to understand. I know that she has had enough when she has chased a ball but does not bring it back to me. This exercise can take a good 20 minutes. And a tennis ball is just the right size for most dogs. The essentiality of walking a dog the way Anita and I do and its challenges are, I think, superbly captured in this poem:

DOG AROUND THE BLOCK

BY E.B WHITE, AN AMERICAN LAURETTE WHO LIVES IN NEW YORK CITY AND OWNS SEVERAL DOGS

Dog around the block, sniff,
Hydrant sniffing, corner, grating,
Sniffing, always, starting forward,
Backward, dragging, sniffing backward,
Leash at taut, leash at dangle,
Leash in people's feet entangle—
Sniffing dog, apprised of smellings,
Love of life, and fronts of dwellings,
Meeting enemies,
Loving old acquaintance, sniff,
Sniffing hydrant for reminders,
Leg against the wall, raise,
Leaving grating, corner greeting,
Chance for meeting, sniff, meeting,
Meeting, telling, news of smelling,
Nose to tail, tail to nose,
Rigid, careful, pose,
Liking, partly liking, hating,
Then another hydrant, grating,
Leash at taut, leash at dangle,
Tangle, sniff, untangle,
Dog around the block, sniff.

The Joy of Walkies

by Andrew Cotter. *London Sunday Times* 11 July 2021

And even on those occasions when you might not want to head out, you must – because this is one of the most treasured parts of a dog's life. Walks and food are the twin pillars of their existence – barring a snack, the very best thing you can give them is their freedom and a chance to lose themselves in a world of nasal investigation; and, as with most of the things they enjoy, they depend entirely on us since they can't walk on their own. Or at least can't do so in any trustworthy fashion.

DOG WALKERS AND THEIR AVAILABILITY

Whether your dog is an active pup who requires a few miles of jogging a day or a couch potato, exercise and mental stimulation are important for all dogs. So, whether you work long hours, have an exacting schedule or are physically unable to give your dog the required exercise, you might want to hire a dog-walker. Like hiring a babysitter, choosing the right dog-walker is a serious business. They are responsible for your dog's well-being and safety during the time they spend together. Also, you are basically opening up your home to a stranger, so trust is important. You need to be clear on what you want in a dog-walker. Your dog-walker needs to know and understand the behaviour of dogs and how dogs communicate and express things like affection, fear, and stress. And in choosing your dog- walker you must know your dog and what she needs. When out walking, dogs vary in their approach to other dogs. Dog-walkers need to know what the dog owner knows about his dog in this regard.

I describe Posh as a friendly dog and announce this when approaching a strange same-size or smaller dog on a leash. If the dog is bigger than Posh, I try to avoid all contact and start tightening the leash, as a fight always seems to be inevitable. The dog-walker should also know of Posh's bad and infuriating habit of, when close enough, slapping the other dog in the face with her right forepaw.

Between my wife and me and Debbie, we have never needed the services of a dog-walker. But I understand that dog-walkers and potential dog-walkers register themselves on the web and leave their contact details with vets, dog parlours, dog speciality shops, the janitors of large apartment houses and sometimes pharmacies and doctor's surgeries.

The potential dog-walker needs to know how dogs communicate and express their concerns and if the person going to be your dog-walker doesn't understand this, it could be a problem.

And YOU need to know your dog and what she requires and be able to convey it to the potential dog-walker. Some dogs like to sniff and pee on virtually every blade of grass. Others see a squirrel and are off and running. Some welcome a leash, while others can be aggressive and struggle with it. Some dog-walkers walk single dogs at a time and others in a whole pack.

CHAPTER 27

SOME THOUGHTS ABOUT FEEDING YOUR DOG

In my youth, I remember my mother cooking food for the dog but today few people have the time or the inclination to do so. And supermarket shelves are packed with an endless variety of proprietary dog foods, sold in cans or packets. The general expert view is that these are well-balanced and generally of a high-quality. Large dog food companies have their own testing laboratories to check the palatability and suitability for all sizes of dog and at all phases in the dog's life.

An important checkpoint made to me is that the protein level should not be less than 10%. Prompted by this, I looked at what we are currently feeding Posh and the protein level stands at 25%.

There are, of course, three main types of prepared dog food – dry, semi-moist and canned. Nobody I consulted expressed a preference other than to make the point that semi-moist are more acceptable than dry. A general point that I picked up is that a well-balanced diet for a dog is not too different from that for a human being, except that the dog's intestines are not well equipped for handling roughage, so foods like bran and certain vegetables containing an excess of fibre should be avoided.

A point also made to me is that dogs want consistency. Once you have made the right choice of food, stay with it. Dogs don't like variations. Dogs of course digest bones easily and can live almost exclusively upon fresh ones that contain marrow. Splintery bones, such as those of poultry or chops are, however, dangerous. As soon as the bone is cooked it becomes brittle and can splinter. Dogs, because they can produce their own vitamin C, have no need for vegetables and fruits, but can eat them if there is nothing else available. They can also readily digest cooked starchy foods. A final point: the amount of food a dog needs depends upon the amount of exercise it gets.

THE DOG FOOD COMPANIES: WHY THE PUBLICITY?

There was a time when most dog-owners themselves went to the trouble of cooking their dog's food. And while I know of some people who still go to the trouble involved, most of us have come to rely on the supermarket shelves weighed down with a great variety of cans and bags of clinically processed pre-cooked canine-appealing cuisine. That is one reason for celebrating these large dog-food producers. But another is to acknowledge the high levels of research that goes into those tins and packets. A third reason is less obvious. It is the important charitable contribution that these large companies make to dog and animal welfare all over the world. This is not generally recognised and we would like to publicly acknowledge it here.

The following are some of the leading dog food manufacturers and their contact details. Their websites are most informative.

MARS PETCARE – **www.mars.com** Manufacturers PEDIGREE, ROYAL CANIN, WHISKAS and CESAR. High quality science-backed nutrition.

EUKANUBA – SA **www.eukanuba.com**

EUKANUBA – UK www.eukanuba.co.uk 100% complete balanced nutrition

THE PET FOOD SPECIALISTS – UK **www. anfrozennlive.co.uk**

WALTHAM PETCARE – UK **www.waltham.com**

K-9 PET FOODS – SA **www.k9petfoods.net** Ph: +27 (0) 21 551 1544

HEALTHY K9 – UK **www.healthyk9.co.uk**

GENERATION PET – E-mails: **sales@genpet. org** / **doug@genpet.org**

www.genpet.org

OMEGA DOG FOODS - **www.omegapetfoods. com** Available at vet clinics and pet shops.

OPTIMIZOR - **www.optimizordogfood.co.za** Ph: 0860 103 764. Some of the leading brands are Bobtail, Canine Cuisine and Ultra Dog.

HILLS PET NUTRITION – SA **www.hillspet. co.za** Ph: 0800 228 783

HILLS PET NUTRITION – UK **www.hillspet. co.uk**

Purchased at vet clinics and speciality shops.

VETSBRANDS – **www.vetsbrands.co.za** Ph: +27 82 710 2982

IAMS – SA **www.iams.com**

IAMS – UK www.iams.co.uk Developed by nutrionists and vets.

ROXBOX - Cape Town based. Complete wellness for your pet.

www.roxbox.co.za Ph: +27 71 474 7350

PAWSOME RAW – SA. Top Grade Nutrition **www.pawsomeraw.com**

Ph +27 73 420 4760

MONTEGO – SA **www.montego.co.za** Ph: +27 49 891 0825

SUPREME PETFOODS – SA **www.supremepet. co.za**

SUPREME PETFOODS – UK **www.petshop. co.uk**

ULTRA DOG - RCL FOODS Website: **www. ultra-pet.co.za / www.rclfoods.com**

E-mail: **support@petheaven.co.za** Ph: 086 010 3764

MY PET WAREHOUSE – Australia **www. mypetwarehouse.com.au**

CRAVE, High Protein – Australia **www.cravepetfood.com.au**

PET FOOD - Australia – **www.petfoodaustralia.com.au**

DELIVERY HOUND – Australia **www.deliveryhound.com.au**

CHAPTER 28

ROUTINE IN A DOG'S LIFE

Routine is important in our lives as human beings, but it is particularly important as far as dogs are concerned because it is part of the ongoing learning process a dog goes through in adjusting to a human's world. Aside from being emphasised by experts, it is very definitely reflected in Posh's behaviour. In fact, the importance of routine can be demonstrated in her behaviour and the routine she follows and even in the commands she responds to.

A DOG'S MORE SUBTLE EXPECTATIONS

Most of a dog's needs are simple. They need exercise, a balanced diet, shelter and companionship to make them feel happy and secure. So, as one dog trainer says: "Remember, no other creature will react to you as a dog will, so be fair, be firm, forgive him rapidly, and love him well". While this is all pretty obvious, there are some needs a dog has that are less obvious and stem from the dog's past origins, traceable in fact to dogs' connections with wolves.

Like wolves, dogs are pack animals by nature. To be specific, a pack is a group of animals that live together for survival. I saw one such pack of wild dogs (there must have been about 15 in the group) on the Spanish island of

Ibiza. These animals are known as Ibiza Hounds, an off-breed specific to Ibiza. They are actually encouraged by the local government as a tourist attraction and garbage is dumped for them at certain points on the island, but they stay away from human habitation.

Because dogs were domesticated from wolf dogs, they exhibit many pack behaviours similar to the wolf. In both the wolf and dog packs, there is always a number one or *alpha* dog, considered top of the pack. This pack looks to value that individual for leadership, structure and protection. If those functions of the pack do not occur, another alpha dog will challenge for that position.

When we bring a dog into our home, whether there are other animals in the home or not, the entire human family becomes part of their pack. According to the people I have consulted, it is essential that the entire family understand what leadership consists of in your dog's eyes, and a pup needs to know his place, his limits and the rules of the household from the beginning.

CHAPTER 29

RESPONSIBLE DOG OWNERSHIP

Dog ownership means more than simply loving your dog. Dog ownership is a serious commitment that takes time and energy. So, before you decide to take on a dog, make sure you can meet your dog's basic needs. There are some extremely important rules of responsible dog ownership you need to know.

One: When you get a dog, you commit for the long haul. When you decided to get a dog you are committing to loving care for as much as 12 to 15 years, even more for some of the smaller breeds.

Two: Make time for your dog. Bonding is not something you can do once and call it finished. Maintaining the bond is a lifelong process.

Three: Provide proper identification. All dogs should wear a collar at all times, with current identification to include your name, phone number and a back-up number. Consider microchipping your dog for an added layer of protection.

Four: Spay and neuter. Millions of pets are euthanised each year because of pet overpopulation. If you do not have your dog spayed or neutered, you may be contributing to this problem.

Five: Keep your dog healthy. Always provide plenty of fresh drinking water and an appropriate amount of quality nutrition for your dog. A place of shelter and comfort is also important for your dog's physical and mental wellness, and exercise is a must. Regular visits to your vet are essential because they can help you prevent serious health problems.

Six: Train your dog. A well-behaved and properly socialised dog is less likely to upset people and other pets in public places and will be more welcome at gatherings. If your dog's misbehaviour results in any sort of accident, injury or similar incident, you will be held fully responsible for that behaviour.

Seven: Make sure you can afford to take care of the animal, food, shelter and veterinary bills. Consider Pet Insurance for those unforeseen hazards and traumas.

Eight: Respect others. Give dog owners a good name by following these rules:-

* Keep your dog on a leash or in a fenced-in yard when outdoors. If you live where it's legal to let your dog off-leash, you should supervise it at all times.

* Pick up after your dog and dispose of it appropriately. No one wants to step in or smell that "gift" your dog has left behind.

* Do not leave a barking dog outdoors. Continuous barking is not only unfair to your dog, but is also rude and annoying to neighbours. There is always a good reason for the dog continuously barking.

CHAPTER 30

ADVOCATE MARK NOWITZ, A SOUTH AFRICAN AND INTERNATIONAL PRACTISING ADVOCATE WHO HAS BEEN A PUG OWNER FOR OVER 30 YEARS, HAS CONTRIBUTED TO THE LEGAL ASPECTS THAT FOLLOW.

SOUTH AFRICA: INJURIES CAUSED BY A DOG – DOG OWNER OBLIGATIONS

The recently widely-publicised instance of a little girl losing her hand as a consequence of a dog bite and the instance of two pit bulls attacking an elderly woman and her dog, sharply focus attention on this particular challenge to dog ownership. The dog's owner in a biting incident can be held liable both for civil damages and criminally.

A victim of an attack by a dog has a civil claim against the owner of the dog, as a result of being bitten, which could include special damages (like to property and medical expenses) and damages (for pain and suffering, loss of amenities of life, disability and disfigurement).

In terms of the Animal Matters Act, criminal actions can be brought against an owner whose dog, as a result of the owner's negligence, has caused injury to another person. If successful, the owner may be sentenced to a fine or to imprisonment for a period not exceeding two years. In South African law, which has a strong Roman law base, a dog owner can be held liable in terms of the *actio* **de** *pauperie* for damage caused by a dog without there being any fault on the part of the owner. The conditions in which the *actio* **de** *pauperie* will apply are spelt out very clearly (ownership, the dog being a domesticated animal and acting contrary to the nature of such and causation) as are the defences available to a dog owner who finds himself / herself in this predicament.

As far as the dog owner is concerned, he needs to prove:

1. the dog was provoked by the victim, a third party or another animal; or
2. a third party in charge or in control of the dog at the time negligently failed to prevent the dog from injuring the victim; or
3. the unlawful presence of the victim on the premises opened the victim to risk; or
4. the victim knew of the risk of sustaining injury from the dog and voluntarily accepted that risk; or
5. the existence of an indemnity, which absolves the dog owner of liability.

SOUTH AFRICA: HOW MANY DOGS CAN YOU KEEP?

The Animal Protection Act of 1962 sets out regulations for all South African pet owners. Those who choose not to follow these rules could receive a penalty fine of up to R4 000 and can even face imprisonment for a period of 12 months depending on the severity of the action. The Act stipulates the number of dogs you are allowed to keep according to the type of property you own. While each region will have its own by-laws in this regard, most subscribe to the following restrictions for dogs over six months of age: a maximum of two dogs may be kept in a dwelling-unit (sectional title); three dogs are allowed to be kept in a dwelling-house (a freestanding property); four dogs are allowed to be kept in a large dwelling-house (a property on a plot exceeding 600m2) and six dogs may be kept on an agricultural property.

AUSTRALIA: A DOG OWNER'S LEGAL OBLIGATIONS

Australia is, of course, a federation and the power to regulate the management of dogs in their areas is transferred to local councils by way of the Dog and Cat Management Act of 1995. The powers granted local councils and their officials are extensive and include destruction orders in respect of Dangerous Dogs, Menacing Dogs, Nuisance Dogs and Barking Dogs. Refusal to cooperate with such an order carries a maximum penalty of AU\$ 5 000 and an assault on such an official, a maximum of AU\$ 10 000 or two years' imprisonment.

AUSTRALIA: HOW MANY DOGS CAN YOU KEEP?

The number of dogs you can own in Australia varies from state to state, but the rules are essentially the same. Take for example the state of Queensland. Within Brisbane you are only allowed to keep two domestic dogs within your home. If you wish to keep more than this, you will need to apply for a domestic dog permit. This permit will allow you to keep up to 14 dogs, with no more than four being over the age of three months unless you are a licensed breeder. There are certain circumstances where you are unlikely to be granted a permit:-

* If the animal lives in a premise which is not a single-detached dwelling, such as a townhouse or unit.

* If the premises for the animal to live on is less than 400 m^2.

* If you have been denied permission to hold a similar permit from another local government.

* If you are not a breeder and the dogs in question for the application have not been desexed.

If you are planning to keep more than two dogs for racing, breeding, sale or show, you will need to apply for a separate breeder or show permit.

UK: LEGAL OBLIGATIONS OF DOG OWNERS

Dog owners in the UK are obviously subject to the responsible ownership provisions listed above. In addition, however, they are subject to the provisions which relate to responsibility for their dog's behaviour.

UK: HOW MANY DOGS CAN YOU KEEP?

There is no limit to how many dogs you can have on your own property, as long as you can look after them and give them the time they need. There are instances on the web of persons having eight and ten dogs in their private homes. But bear in mind that the law now requires every dog in the UK to be microchipped.

Dangerous Dogs. Some types of dogs are illegal to own, breed, sell, abandon, or give away.

The four banned types are:

*Pitbull Terrier *Japanese Tosa *Dogo Argentino * Fila Brazileiro

If you own any one of these types of dogs, a court can make a destruction order (in which case the dog will be euthanised), or the court can decide that the owner is suitable and that your dog doesn't pose a risk to the general public. In such cases, the court can make a "contingent destruction order". This means your dog will be exempt and allowed to stay with you under strict conditions, including neutering, microchipping, tattooing with a unique identifier, third party insurance and registration on the index of Exempted Dogs. The dog will need to be muzzled in public and kept on a lead. Failing to comply with these strict conditions could lead to seizure of your dog and prosecution.

Dangerously Out of Control

It is against the law to let any type of dog be dangerously out of control anywhere, such as in a public place or in a private place, for example a neighbour's house or garden, or in the owner's home.

Your Dog is Considered Dangerously Out of Control if it injures someone or makes someone worried that it might injure them. If the dog is considered to be out of control:

*You may receive an unlimited fine or be sent to prison for up to 6 months (or both).

*You may be disallowed from owning a dog in the future and your dog may be put down.

*If you encourage your dog to injure someone, you can be sent to prison for up to five years or fined (or both). If you deliberately use your dog to injure someone, you could be charged with "malicious wounding".

Mandatory Microchipping

As of 2016, the law requires that all dogs in England, Wales, Scotland and Northern Ireland be microchipped, and the owner's details must be registered on one of the authorised databases (such as petlog). This applies to all dogs and puppies over the age of eight weeks.

Exemptions are available if a veterinarian believes there is a valid health reason not to microchip a dog. All dogs must have an appropriate collar and tag with the owner's name and address on it when in a public place, even if the dog is microchipped.

If your dog is attacked by another dog, it is an offence for a dog owner to allow his dog to be "dangerously out of control". This means that if another dog attacks your dog, and if you fear that it will injure you if you attempt to stop it, and the owner of the other dog fails to control their pet, you can take them to court. The court will determine whether an offence has been committed and you have the right to reclaim costs resulting from damage to your dog and costs incurred by you in respect to your medical and veterinary responses.

Incidentally, by-laws in Cape Town vary, but are heading towards enforcing compulsory microchipping and registration.

CHAPTER 31

TEN MOST BELOVED DOGS IN LITERATURE BY KATHERINE RIPLEY

Since dogs are an important part of our lives, dogs are also an important part of our literature. They accompany us on our adventures and protect us from our adversaries. Sometimes, dogs are the stars of the stories. Here's a list of the most beloved dogs in literature:

1. **Lassie:** Lassie is by far the most famous canine movie star. Her story, though, was based on the 1940 novel *Lassie Come Home*, in which this faithful **Collie goes on an epic journey to** reunite with the little boy she loves. The story touched so many hearts that it turned into one of Hollywood's biggest franchises.

2. **Toto:** *The Wonderful Wizard of Oz* was a children's book by L. Frank Baum before it was a movie, and neither would be complete without Dorothy's **Cairn Terrier**, Toto. Toto serves as Dorothy's confidant on her journey through the land of Oz.

3. **Clifford:** *Clifford the Big Red Dog* was first published in 1963, and children still love the series of these books today. Clifford, the gentle giant, carries around his owner, Emily, and hangs out with his two best dog friends, Cleo and T-Bone. The book series was turned into a television show.

4. **Buck:** In *The Call of the Wild*, Jack London tells a vivid, heart-wrenching story about a **St. Bernard-**Scotch Shepherd mix named Buck that is kidnapped and forced to become a sled dog. Buck endures various forms of mistreatment, but triumphs thanks to his resilience and some help from a kind human. Buck's story is not for the faint of heart, but it is truly unforgettable.

5. **Old Yeller:** Even if you haven't read *Old Yeller* by Fred Gipson, or seen the movie adaptation, you've surely heard of the story. Old Yeller, a **Labrador Retriever-Mastiff mix, bravely defends his owners against wolves, bears and other wild animals. In the mother of all sad endings, Old Yeller gets rabies while protecting the family from a rabid wolf, and he** has to be put down.

6. **Nana:** In J.M. Barrie's *Peter Pan* and its Disney film adaptation, a **Newfoundland named Nana is in charge of taking care of the children of the Darling**

family. **Obviously, she's more trustworthy than a human nanny would be.**

7. **Winn-Dixie:** Kate DiCamillo's *Because of Winn-Dixie* is the story of a girl and a dog in need. The protagonist, 10-year-old Opal, was abandoned by her mother at a young age and has trouble making friends. After she rescues a stray mixed-breed dog and names him Winn-Dixie, her new dog serves as her wingman and helps her make friends.

   Fun fact: Although the book portrays Winn-Dixie as a mixed-breed, in the **film adaptation they actually used a Berger Picard**! As the **Berger Picard Club of America explains**, "It is this breed's rustic, tousled appearance that has fooled many people into thinking Winn-Dixie is just a mutt."

8. **Tock:** *The Phantom Tollbooth* **is a magical adventure story that follows the protagonist, Milo, through "the Lands Beyond"**. Tock, a giant talking dog with a clock on his body, guides Milo on his journey.

9. **Fang:** Fang is Hagrid's pet dog in the Harry Potter book series. Despite his **large size**, Fang is afraid of almost everything, but he is still willing to accompany the students on their dangerous journeys and protect his master from threatening spells.

10. Argos: Argos is Odysseus' dog in *The Odyssey*. **He plays a small role in the book, but an important one. When Odysseus returns home to Ithaca after 20 years, Argos is the only one who** recognises him. Now that his master is home, Argos can die in peace. Argos is one of the first dogs ever to be named in Western literature, and he's proof that dogs have been man's best friend for as long as we can remember.

ADDITIONAL READING AND CLINICAL INFORMATION ON DOGS -

The Puppy Listener by Jan Fennell
Raising A Puppy by Victoria Stilwell
Short Guide to A Happy Dog by Cesar Millan
You & Your Dog by David Taylor
Talking with Dogs and Cats by Tim Link
The Philosopher And The Wolf by Mark Rowlands
Don't Shoot The Dog by Karen Pryor

Posh and Friends

I'LL NEVER FORGET A DOG NAMED BEAU

BY JIMMY STEWART

https://youtu.be/mwGnCIdHQH0

He never came to me when I would call
Unless I had a tennis ball,
Or he felt like it,
But mostly he didn't come at all.
When he was young
He never learned to heel
Or sit or stay, He did things his way.
Discipline was not his bag
But when you were with him things sure didn't drag.

He'd dig up a rosebush just to spite me,
And when I'd grab him, he'd turn and bite me.
He bit lots of folks from day to day,
The delivery boy was his favourite prey.
The gas man wouldn't read our meter,
He said we owned a real man-eater.

He set the house on fire
But the story's long to tell.

Suffice it to say that he survived
And the house survived as well.
On the evening walks, and Gloria took him,
He was always first out the door.
The Old One and I brought up the rear
Because our bones were sore.
He would charge up the street with Mom hanging on,
What a beautiful pair they were!

And if it was still light and the tourists were out,
They created a bit of a stir.
But every once in a while, he would stop in his tracks
And with a frown on his face look around.

It was just to make sure that the Old One was there
And would follow him where he was bound.
We are early-to-bedders at our house -- I guess I'm the first to
retire.
And as I'd leave the room he'd look at me
And get up from his place by the fire.
He knew where the tennis balls were upstairs,
And I'd give him one for a while.
He would push it under the bed with his nose
And I'd fish it out with a smile.
And before very long
He'd tire of the ball

And be asleep in his corner
In no time at all.

And there were nights when I'd feel him
Climb upon our bed
And lie between us,
And I'd pat his head.
And there were nights when I'd feel this stare
And I'd wake up and he'd be sitting there
And I'd reach out my hand and stroke his hair.
And sometimes I'd feel him sigh and I think I know the
reason why.

He would wake up at night
And he would have this fear
Of the dark, of life, of lots of things,
And he'd be glad to have me near.
And now he's dead.
And there are nights when I think I feel him
Climb upon our bed and lie between us,
And I pat his head.
And there are nights when I think I feel that stare
And I reach out my hand to stroke his hair,
But he's not there.
Oh, how I wish that wasn't so,
I'll always love a dog named Beau.

As always, I thank my darling wife Anita for sharing Posh with me, Jane for so brilliantly understanding Posh, and Debbie for taking such good care of Posh.